Civil Engineering

Practice Examination #2

Timothy J. Nelson, PE

Civil Engineering Practice Examination #2
Timothy J. Nelson

To report errors in this text, contact: tim@engineeringvideos.net

13-Digit ISBN: 9780615887838

EngineeringVideos.Net
Copyright © 2013

Table of Contents

Introduction

Civil Engineering Practice Examination #2 provides 40 multiple-choice civil engineering exam problems to help civil engineers prepare for their professional licensing examinations.

Breadth Exam Topics

Civil Engineering Practice Examination #2 follows the specifications of the breadth examination (morning session), as defined by the National Council of Examiners for Engineering and Surveying (NCEES). This exam includes 8 questions from each of the 5 civil engineering sub-disciplines tested during the morning session of the Civil PE Exam:

- Water Resources and Environmental Engineering (8 questions)
- Geotechnical Engineering (8 questions)
- Structural Engineering (8 questions)
- Construction (8 questions)
- Transportation Engineering (8 questions)

The questions in this exam are mixed up and in no particular order; they are not grouped or identified by their sub-discipline. Within each sub-discipline, different topics and kinds of problems are presented. For example, water resources and environmental engineering problems may involve open channel flow, water quality, groundwater, pumps, hydraulics, etc.

Each problem in this exam provides four possible answers. For each problem there is only one correct answer. The calculated answer will be equal to, or closest to one of the four multiple choice answers provided.

Each problem is a separate and complete problem; the solution to one problem does not depend on the solution to a different problem. The problems can be solved in any order, all are quantitative, there are no 'word problems', and there are no trick problems. It is possible however, that more information will be provided than is necessary to solve the problem.

Practice examination problems in this text are not extremely hard or extremely easy; they are designed to be similar in nature and level of difficulty as the breadth portion of the Civil PE Exam.

How this Book is Organized

This book is divided into three sections: Problems, Detailed Solutions and Quick Solutions.

Problems: The Problems Section lists all 40 problems, three problems per page. All problems are multiple choice.

Detailed Solutions: The Detailed Solutions Section includes a restatement of the problem, followed by an analysis showing one way to determine the correct answer.

Quick Solutions: The Quick Solutions Section only includes the letter corresponding to the correct answer (A, B, C or D).

Problem Layout

Each problem is divided into 4 parts: Find, Given, Analysis, and Answer.

Find: The parameter to be determined/calculated is identified and labeled.

Given: The variables are identified and labeled; usually a figure is provided. Four possible answers are given.

Analysis: The problem is solved. Equations, figures and tables are positioned on the left side of the page, while notes and commentary are positioned on the right side of the page. The analysis concludes by identifying the value of the parameter to be determined/calculated.

Answer: The letter (A, B, C or D) corresponding to the correct answer.

How to Use this Exam

Civil Engineering Practice Examination #2 should be used as an assessment tool for the test-taker to evaluate his or her strengths and weaknesses within the field of civil engineering.

Although the Detailed Solutions section explains the equations and process used to solve each problem, this practice examination does not teach the topics of civil engineering from scratch.

Notation and Terminology

Equations and inequalities are labeled and numbered using the notations shown below. Relationships involving 'at least' ($\geq$) and 'at most' ($\leq$) are considered inequalities. Not all equations or inequalities are labeled.

$$\text{equation} = \text{eq.}\#$$
$$\text{inequality} = \text{ieq.}\#$$

Figures in this examination are not necessarily drawn to scale, especially when a scaled drawing in the problem statement would give away the solution. It is advisable to rely primarily on the numbers and labels to understand each problem and solution.

Typically 3 or 4 significant figures are maintained when the problem is solved in the 'Detailed Solutions' Section. For a multiple choice examination, greater precision is rarely necessary.

There may be more than one method to determine the correct answer. The method used to solve each problem in this text is not necessarily the only way to determine the solution.

About the Author

Tim Nelson works as a Civil Engineer and Web Developer in Sacramento, California. He earned his Bachelor's and Master's Degrees in Civil Engineering in 2005 and 2007, respectively. Tim passed the Civil PE Exam in the State of California, in 2009.

Afterwards, Tim built the website EngineeringVideos.Net and created hundreds of short video example problems covering the various sub-disciplines of Civil Engineering.

Civil Engineering Practice Examination #2 is an extension of Tim's effort to help others successfully prepare for and pass the NCEES Civil Engineering Licensing Examination.

Section 1: Problems

(page intentionally left blank)

Problem #1

Find: A ← the total area of the roof

Given:

$\theta_A = 25°$ $\theta_B = 15°$

the angle the roof makes with the horizon

$l_A = 25 \,[ft]$ } the length of
$l_B = 33 \,[ft]$ } parts A and B

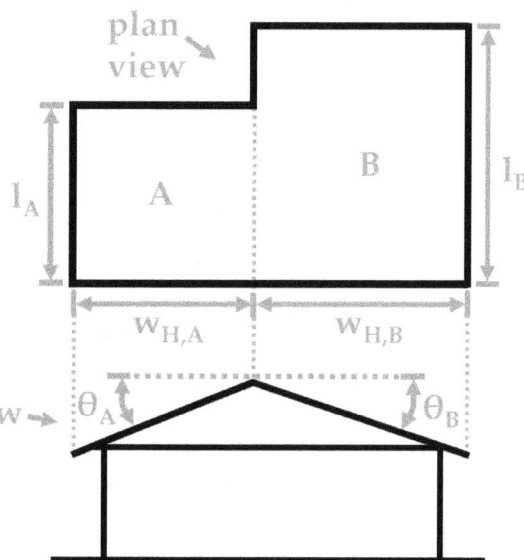

plan view

B

A

l_A l_B

$w_{H,A}$ $w_{H,B}$

profile view → θ_A θ_B

$w_{H,A} = 15 \,[ft]$
$w_{H,B} = 20 \,[ft]$

the horizontal width of part A and part B

A) 978 [ft²]
B) 1,035 [ft²]
C) 1,065 [ft²]
D) 1,110 [ft²]

Problem #2

Find: Flow Classification

the channel side slopes are 1.5:1 (horizontal:vertical)

Given:

$Q = 15 \,[m^3/s]$ ← flow rate

$d = 1 \,[m]$ ← depth of flow

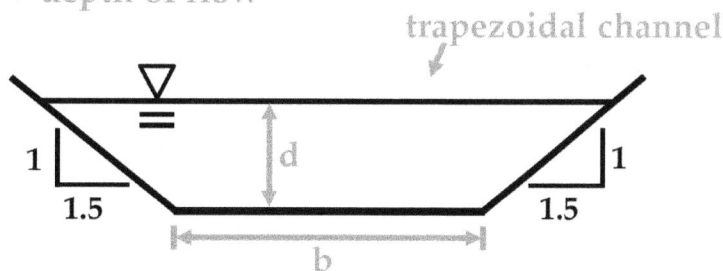

$b = 3 \,[m]$ ← base width

trapezoidal channel

1 / 1.5   d   1 / 1.5

b

A) supercritical
B) critical
C) subcritical
D) not enough information

Problem #3

Find: S ← saturation of the soil sample

Given:

$SG = 2.69$ ← specific gravity of the solid material

$V_T = 1 \,[cm^3]$ ← total volume

$e = 0.70$ ← void ratio

$wc = 12\%$ ← water content

properties of the soil sample

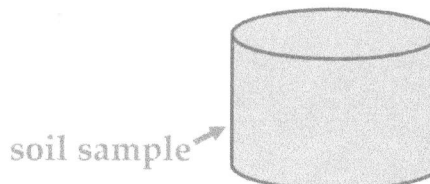

soil sample

A) 12%
B) 19%
C) 41%
D) 46%

Problem #4

Find: I ← the interior angle of the curve

Given:

$L_{AB}=150\,[m]$ ← the length along the larger curve

$L_{XC}=123\,[m]$ ← the radius of the the smaller curve

$2*L_{XC}=L_{YB}$

the two horizontal curves have the same interior angle

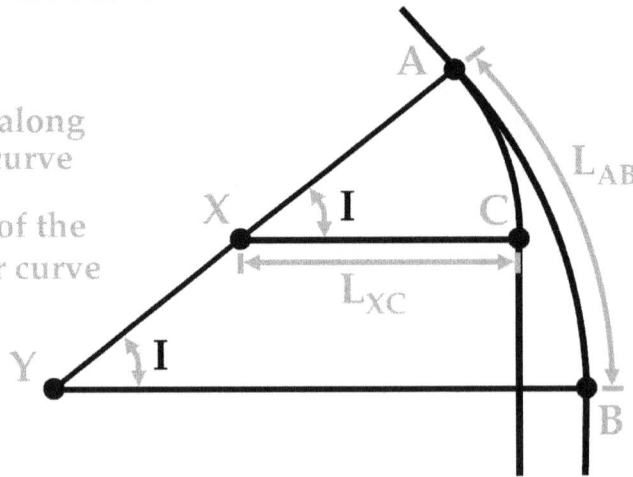

A) 30°
B) 35°
C) 40°
D) 45°

Problem #5

Find: $y_{(x=L)}$ ← the vertical deflection at the end of the cantilever beam

Given:

$L_1=6\,[ft]$ ⎫ length along
$L_2=6\,[ft]$ ⎭ the beam

$w=7\,[k/ft]$ ← uniform load along length L_2 of the beam.

$I=1,400\,[in^4]$ ← area moment of inertia

$E=2.9*10^7\,[lb/in^2]$ ← elastic modulus

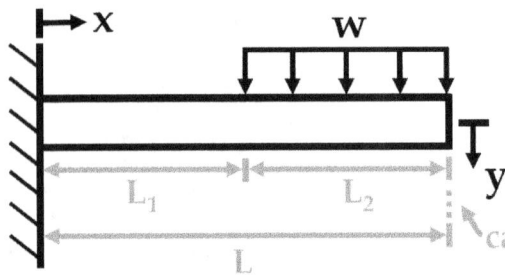

cantilever beam

A) 0.11 [in]
B) 0.66 [in]
C) 0.77 [in]
D) 0.88 [in]

Problem #6

Find: q_{ult} ← ultimate bearing capacity of the square footing

Given:

$d=0\,[ft]$ ← depth of footing beneath soil surface

no groundwater table

$\phi=20°$ ← friction angle

$c=0\,[lb/ft^2]$ ← cohesion

$B=W=8\,[ft]$
base length and width of the square footing

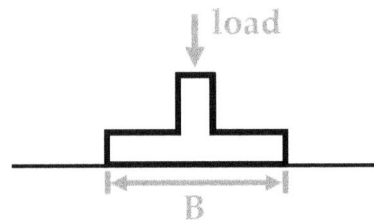

$\gamma=115\,[lb/ft^3]$ ← unit weight

A) 1,000 [lb/ft²]
B) 2,000 [lb/ft²]
C) 3,000 [lb/ft²]
D) 4,000 [lb/ft²]

Problem #7

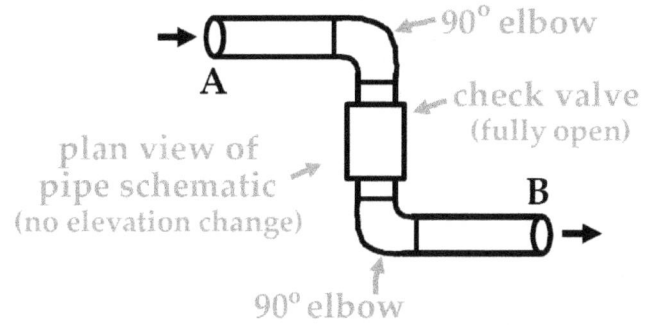

90° elbow

A

check valve
(fully open)

B

plan view of
pipe schematic
(no elevation change)

90° elbow

Find: P_B ← the pressure at point B

Given: $Q = 0.20 [ft^3/s]$ ← flow rate

$L = 60 [ft]$ ← pipe length

$P_A = 80 [lb_f/in^2]$ ← pressure at point A

$C = 100$ ← Hazen-Williams roughness coefficient

$k_{valve} = 2.3$ ⎫ minor headloss coefficients for
$k_{90°} = 0.9$ ⎭ a check valve and 90° elbow

$d = 4 [in]$ ← pipe diameter

water
fluid flowing
through the pipe

A) $75.2 [lb_f/in^2]$
B) $76.7 [lb_f/in^2]$
C) $78.1 [lb_f/in^2]$
D) $79.6 [lb_f/in^2]$

Problem #8

Find: A ← area of coating on a single pile

Given:

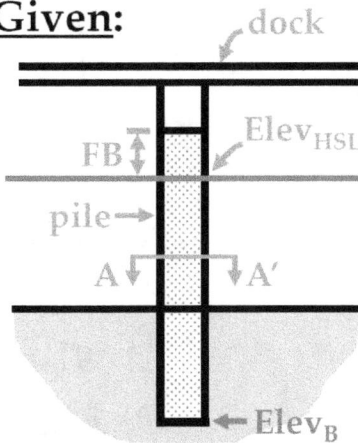

dock

coating covers the entire pile up
to the high sea level elevation
plus the freeboard height, and base

$Elev_{HSL} = 125.7 [ft]$
high sea level

$Elev_B = 86.4 [ft]$
elevation at pile base

FB ← ElevHSL
pile →
A ↓ ↓ A'

← ElevB

FB = 4 [ft] ← freeboard

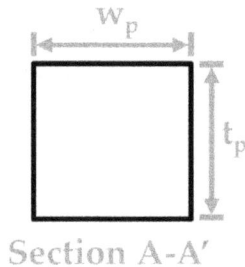

w_p

t_p

Section A-A'

$w_p = 2.5 [ft]$
pile width

$t_p = 2.5 [ft]$
pile thickness

A) $245 [ft^2]$
B) $271 [ft^2]$
C) $433 [ft^2]$
D) $439 [ft^2]$

Problem #9

Find: SRR ← the superelevation runoff rate

Given:

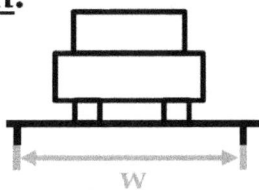

w

$STA_A = 150 [m]$

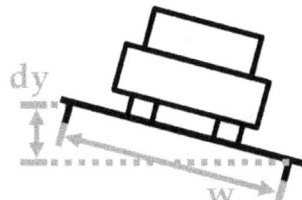

dy

w

$STA_B = 216 [m]$

w = 3.8 [m]
lane width

$R = 80 [m]$ ← radius of the horizontal curve

$dy = 0.33 [m]$ ← the superelevation at station B

A) 1/180
B) 1/200
C) 1/220
D) 1/240

Civil Engineering Practice Examination #2

Problem #10

Find: LL ←liquid limit

Given:

$$M_{Dish}=0.13\,[lb] \leftarrow \text{mass of the dish}$$

Liquid Limit Test Data

Sample	$M_{Moist\ Soil\ \&\ Dish}$	$M_{Dry\ Soil\ \&\ Dish}$	# Turns
1	2.41 [lb]	1.68 [lb]	12
2	2.45 [lb]	1.82 [lb]	22
3	2.39 [lb]	1.88 [lb]	37

A) 28
B) 34
C) 41
D) 48

Problem #11

Find: h_b ←beam height

Given:

$L=9\,[ft]$ ←beam length

$w_b=6\,[in]$ ←beam width

$E=2.9*10^7\,[lb/in^2]$ ←elastic modulus

$y_{max}=0.059\,[in]$

↑
maximum deflection in the beam caused by the loading

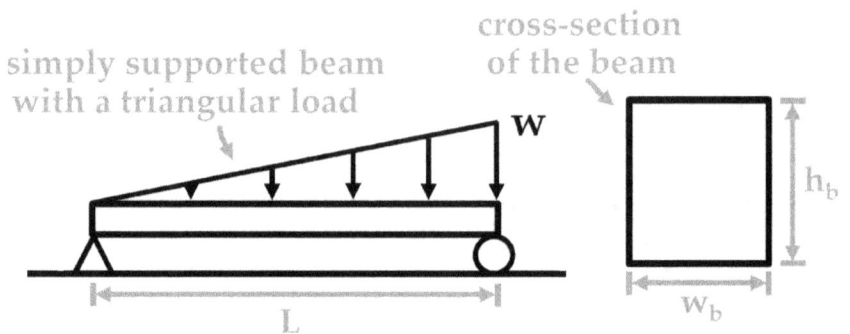

simply supported beam with a triangular load

cross-section of the beam

$w=20\,[k/ft]$

↑
loading at the far right end of the beam

A) 6 [in]
B) 8 [in]
C) 9 [in]
D) 12 [in]

Problem #12

Find: F_R ←the reaction force required to hold the vane stationary

Given:

$Q=0.25\,[m^3/s]$

↑
flow rate

$v=15\,[m/s]$ ← velocity of flow

$\varrho=750\,[kg/m^3]$ ←density of the fluid

$\theta=38°$ ←deflection angle

vane

neglect all forces caused by gravity and (static) pressure

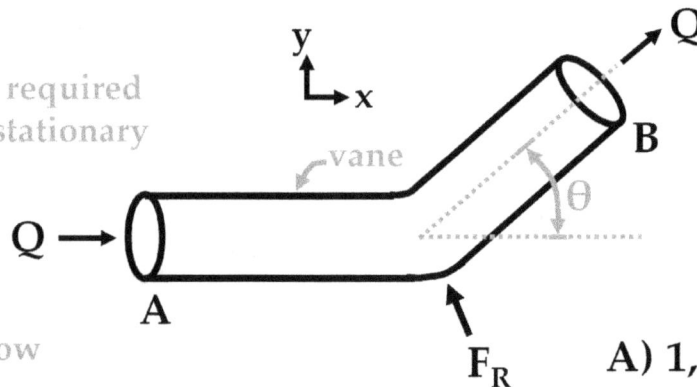

A) 1,730 [N]
B) 1,830 [N]
C) 5,030 [N]
D) 5,320 [N]

Problem #13

<u>Find:</u> $s_{2,s}$ ← stopping distance of vehicle 2

<u>Given:</u>   G=0 ← grade

$v_{1,i}=25\,[mi/hr]$ ← initial velocity of vehicle 1

$t_{1,r}=1.5\,[s]$ ← reaction time of vehicle 1 $v_{2,i}=55\,[mi/hr]$

$s_{1,b}=114.6\,[ft]$ ← stopping distance
of vehicle 1   initial velocity
of vehicle 2

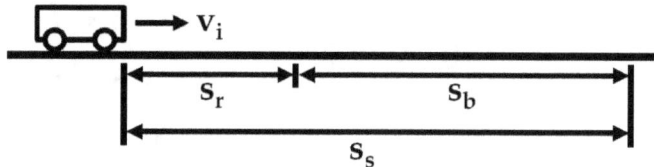

$t_{2,r}=2.0\,[s]$

reaction time
of vehicle 2

A) 250 [ft]
B) 390 [ft]
C) 560 [ft]
D) 720 [ft]

Problem #14

<u>Find:</u> The Critical Path

<u>Given:</u>

$ES_A=1$

the early start
of Activity A

$ES_B=1$

the early start
of Activity B

ID	Duration	Pred
A	1	-
B	4	-
C	5	A
D	1	A,B
E	8	B,D
F	6	C
G	4	D,E,F

← predecessor
activities

A) A-C-F-G
B) A-D-E-G
C) B-D-E-G
D) B-D-G

Problem #15

<u>Find:</u> F_{GC} ← the force in member GC

<u>Given:</u>

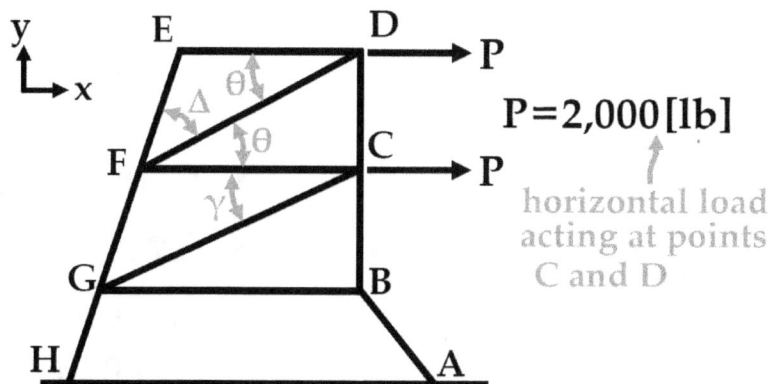

$\theta=37.6°$ ⎫
$\Delta=49.3°$ ⎬ interior angles
$\gamma=32.0°$ ⎭ of the structure

$P=2,000\,[lb]$

horizontal load
acting at points
C and D

A) 4,180 [lb] (tension)
B) 4,620 [lb] (tension)
C) 4,180 [lb] (compression)
D) 4,620 [lb] (compression)

Civil Engineering Practice Examination #2

Problem #16

Find: Q_p ← peak runoff flow rate

Given: 20-year storm event

total runoff area

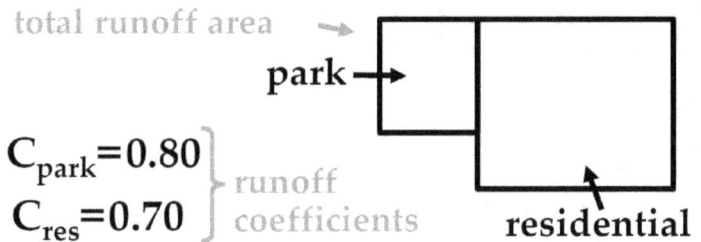

park →

residential

i [in/hr] $d=60$ [min] ← storm duration

$C_{park}=0.80$ ⎫ runoff
$C_{res}=0.70$ ⎭ coefficients

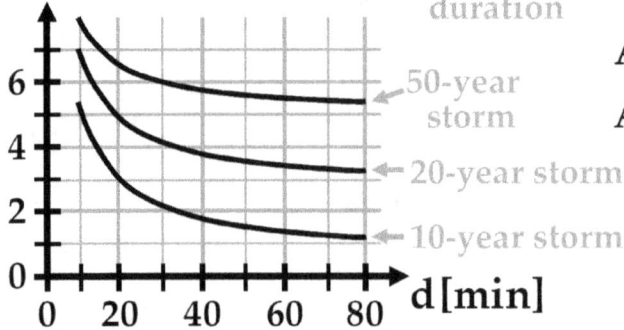

50-year storm

20-year storm

10-year storm

$A_{park}=5$ [acres] ⎫ watershed areas
$A_{res}=15$ [acres] ⎭

$t_c=40$ [min]

time of concentration

A) 17 [ft³/s]

B) 38 [ft³/s]

C) 51 [ft³/s]

D) 85 [ft³/s]

Problem #17

assume there is no swell or shrinkage of the soil

Find: C ← total cost of transporting soil

Given: R=$0.01 [ft⁻⁴] ← unit cost of transporting soil per cubic foot volume, per foot of distance traveled

$w=15$ [ft]

constant width of the soil pile and fill pit (into and out of the page)

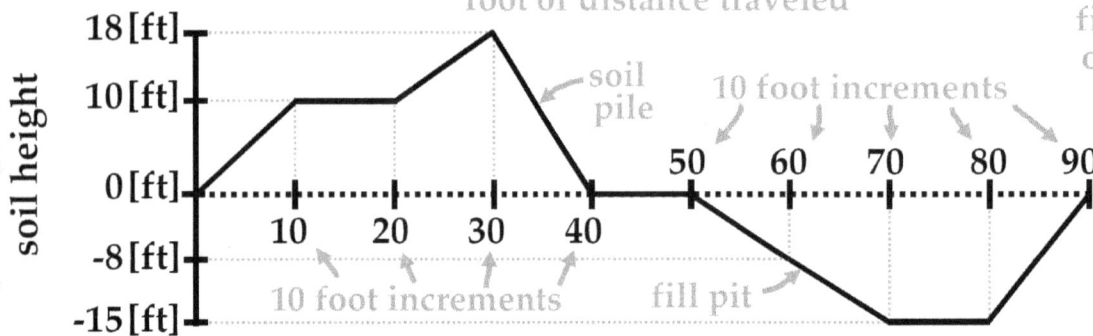

soil height

soil pile

10 foot increments

10 foot increments   fill pit

A) $190

B) $1,550

C) $2,800

D) $5,670

Problem #18

$E=2.9*10^7$ [lb/in²]

elastic modulus

Find: P_{cr} ← the critical axial force of the column

Given:

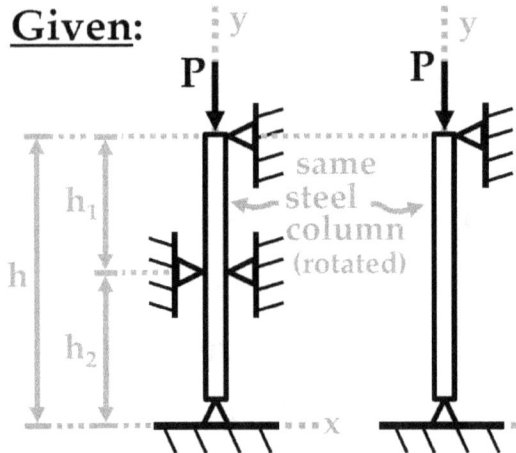

P

P

same steel column (rotated)

$L=2$ [in] ⎫ the length and width
$w=1$ [in] ⎭ of the steel column

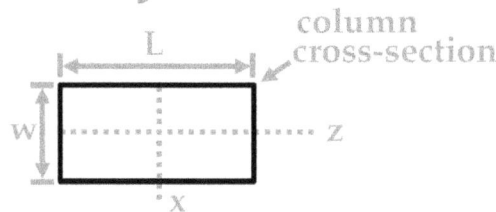

column cross-section

L

w

z

x

all connections are pin connections

$h_1=10$ [ft]

$h_2=12$ [ft]

A) 2,300 [lb]

B) 2,740 [lb]

C) 3,320 [lb]

D) 5,480 [lb]

Problem #19

Find: I ← the interior angle of the curve

Given:

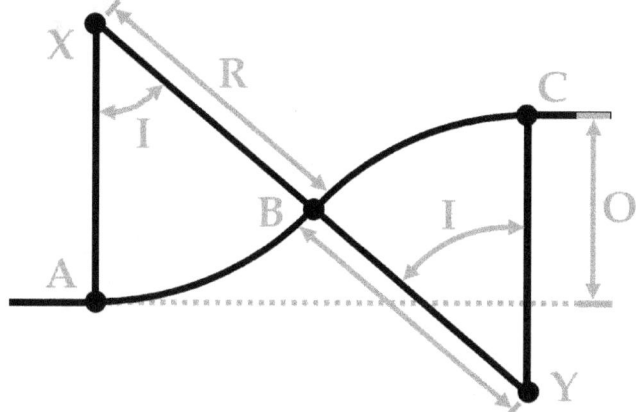

$O=400\,[\text{ft}]$ ← offset distance

$D=2.690°$ ← degree of curve [arc-basis]

← the compound horizontal curves share the same interior angle and radius

A) 25°
B) 30°
C) 35°
D) 40°

Problem #20

Find: V ← the volume of flow beneath the embankment in a 12 hour period

assume steady-state flow conditions apply

Given:

$L=20\,[\text{m}]$ ← length of the dam and aquifer (into and out of the page)

$t=12\,[\text{hr}]$ ← duration

$K=0.015\,[\text{cm/s}]$ ← hydraulic conductivity

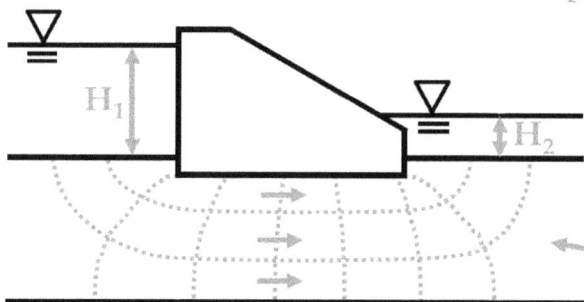

$H_1=5.0\,[\text{m}]$ ← upstream head

$H_2=1.2\,[\text{m}]$ ← downstream head

← flow net

A) 21 [m³]
B) 250 [m³]
C) 1,000 [m³]
D) 25,000 [m³]

Problem #21

Find: i ← the annual interest rate of the investment

Given:

$A_{1-5}=\$-15,000$ ← the annual deposit at the end of years 1 through 5

$F_{15}=\$135,000$ ← the future withdrawal at the end of year 15

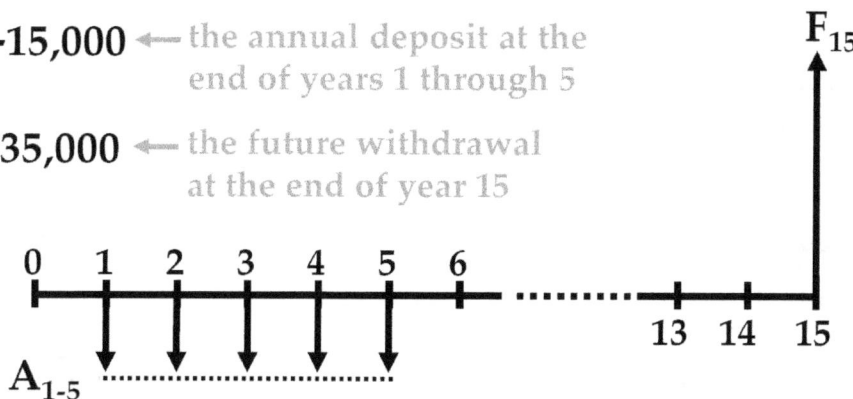

A) 4%
B) 5%
C) 6%
D) 7%

9

Problem #22

Find: P_1 ←the point load acting downward at the end of the circular beam.

Given:

$d=8\,[cm]$ ← the diameter of the beam

$L=31\,[cm]$ ← the length of the beam

$P_2=25\,[N]$ ←the point load acting horizontal at the end of the beam.

$\sigma_A=23{,}470\,[N/m^2]$

the normal stress at point A (in compression)

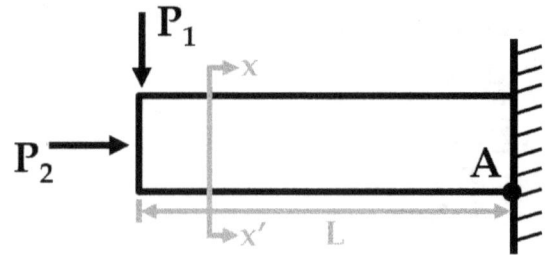

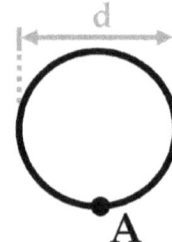

section x-x'

A) 3 [N]
B) 6 [N]
C) 9 [N]
D) 12 [N]

Problem #23

Find: P ←the pump power

Given:

water

$d_A=10\,[in]$ ← inlet diameter

$d_B=6\,[in]$ ← outlet diameter

$z_{AB}=6\,[in]$

vertical distance between the bottom of the two pipes

$P_A=25\,[lb_f/in^2]$ ← inlet pressure

$P_B=60\,[lb_f/in^2]$ ← outlet pressure

$\eta=75\%$

pump efficiency

$Q=1{,}200\,[gal/min]$ ← flow rate

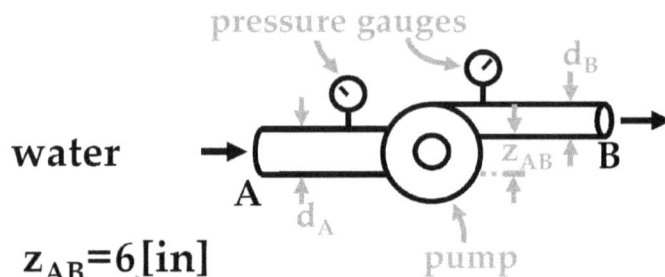

pressure gauges

pump

A) 4 [hp]
B) 14 [hp]
C) 24 [hp]
D) 34 [hp]

Problem #24

Find: Range of Allowable Water Content

Given:

wc	$\gamma_T\,[lb/ft^3]$
0.10	114.8
0.15	126.1
0.20	132.6
0.25	136.9
0.30	133.3

compaction test data

RC=95%

relative compaction

A) 10% - 29%
B) 14% - 25%
C) 17% - 22%
D) 20% - 30%

Problem #25

Find: d_1 ← the inside diameter of the steel shaft

Given:

$E=2*10^{11}[N/m^2]$ ← elastic modulus

$T=50[N*m]$ ← applied torque

$L=1.00[m]$ ← shaft length

$d_2=5[cm]$ ← outer diameter

$\gamma=1.06107*10^{-3}[rad]$ ← torsional deflection

$\mathcal{V}=0.30$ ← Poisson's Ratio

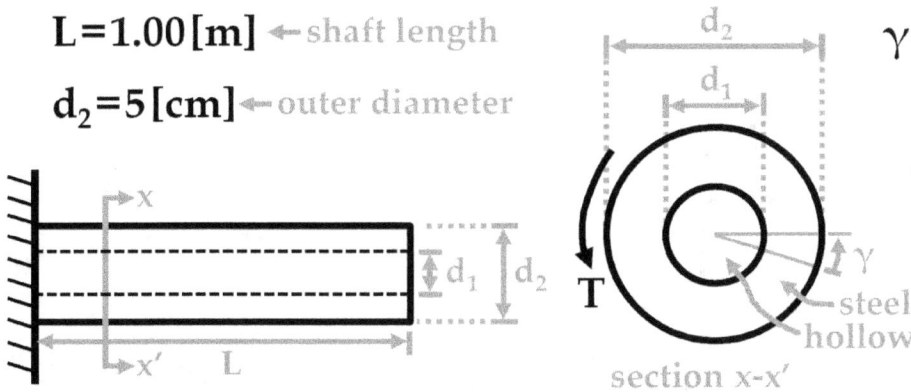

section x-x'

A) 1[cm]

B) 2[cm]

C) 3[cm]

D) 4[cm]

Problem #26

Find: L_{AB} ← the length of the vertical curve

Given:

$STA_A=23+00$ ← the stationing and elevation of point A, the beginning of the vertical curve.

$y_A=191.58[ft]$

the stationing and elevation of point B, the end of the vertical curve.

$STA_B=26+00$

$y_B=196.11[ft]$

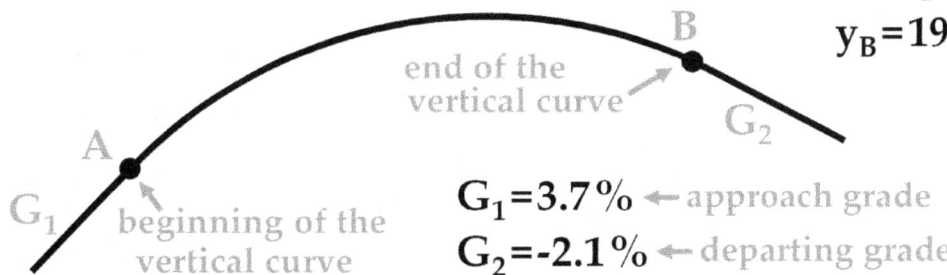

end of the vertical curve

beginning of the vertical curve

$G_1=3.7\%$ ← approach grade

$G_2=-2.1\%$ ← departing grade

A) 400[ft]

B) 500[ft]

C) 600[ft]

D) 700[ft]

Problem #27

Find: T ← the number of truck loads required to remove the excess soil after the terrain elevation is leveled to elevation equals 0 feet

Given:

$w=20[ft]$ ← width of cut pile and fill pit (into and out of the page)

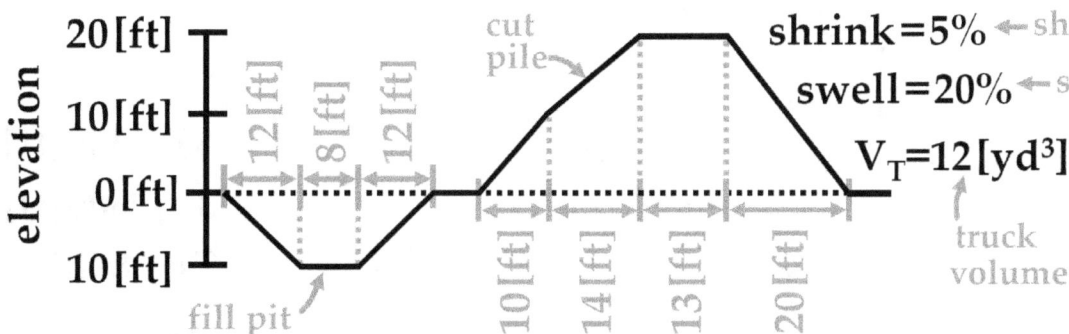

cut pile

fill pit

shrink=5% ← shrinkage factor

swell=20% ← swell factor

$V_T=12[yd^3]$ ← truck volume

A)   30

B)   37

C)   38

D) 1,018

Civil Engineering Practice Examination #2

Problem #28

Find: $BOD_{5,30°C}$ ← the biochemical oxygen demand after 5 days at a temperature of 30°C.

Given:

$BOD_{5,20°C}=210\,[mg/L]$ ← the biochemical oxygen demand after 5 days at a temperature of 20°C.

$K_{d,20°C}=0.23\,[day^{-1}]$ ← deoxygenation rate constant at 20°C.

$\theta=1.047$ ← temperature constant

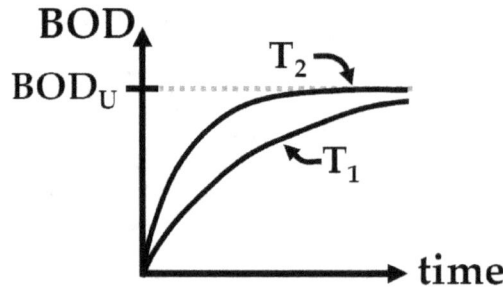

A) 159 [mg/L]

B) 223 [mg/L]

C) 258 [mg/L]

D) 307 [mg/L]

Problem #29

Find: $LL_{B,max}$ ← the maximum live load at point B

Given:

$L_{AB}=6\,[ft]$ ⎫ length along the beam
$L_{BC}=6\,[ft]$ ⎭

$DL_{AC}=2,000\,[lb/ft]$ ← the dead load from point A to point C

$y_{max}=0.040\,[in]$ ← maximum deflection in the beam

$E=2.9*10^7\,[lb/in^2]$ ← elastic modulus

$I=1,650\,[in^4]$ ← area moment of inertia

used load factors

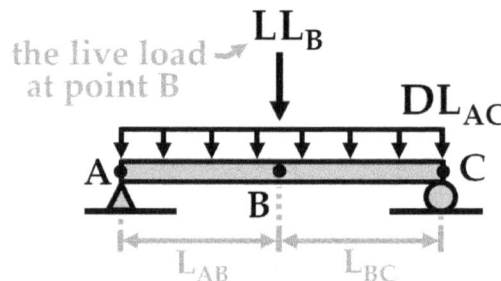

A) 7,980 [lb]

B) 9,770 [lb]

C) 12,770 [lb]

D) 21,000 [lb]

Problem #30

the vehicle drives from point A to point B along the road

Find: C_{AB} ← the major cord from A to B of the horizontal curve

Given:

$v_A=3.4\,[mi/hr]$ ← the velocity of the vehicle at points A and B
$v_B=33.7\,[mi/hr]$

$I=120°$ ← interior angle   road →

$a_{AB}=1\,[ft/s^2]$

constant acceleration of the vehicle between points A and B

the vehicle begins at A, traveling northward

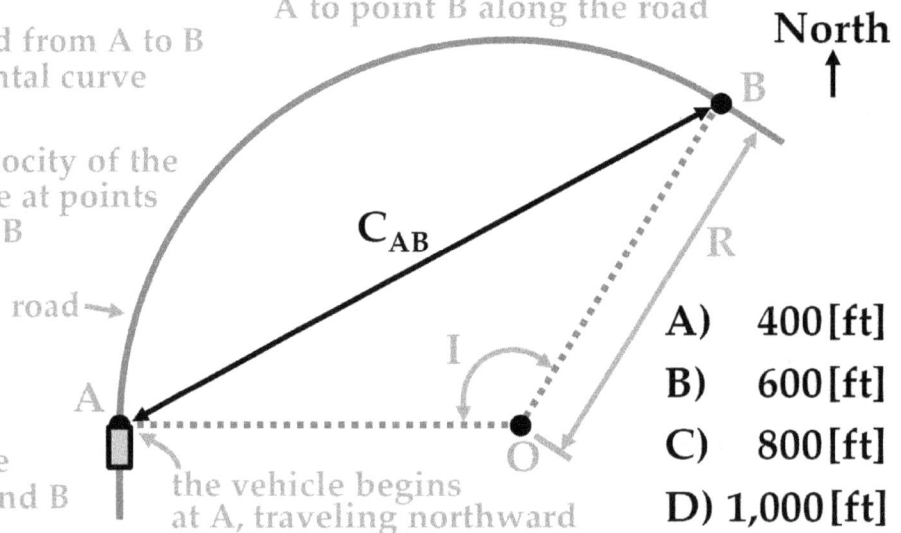

A) 400 [ft]

B) 600 [ft]

C) 800 [ft]

D) 1,000 [ft]

Problem #31

Find: ϱ_c ← ultimate consolidation settlement of the clay layer

Given:

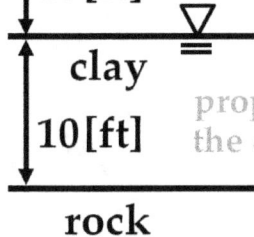

$\Delta\sigma = 300\,[\mathrm{lb/ft^2}]$ ← loading

sand

10 [ft]

$\gamma' = 110\,[\mathrm{lb/ft^3}]$ ← effective unit weight of the sand layer

clay

10 [ft]

properties of → the clay layer

rock

$wc = 25\%$ ← water content

$SG = 2.65$ ← specific gravity

$C_C = 0.70$ ← consolidation index

groundwater table is at the sand-clay interface

clay is normally consolidated

A) 0.11 [ft]
B) 0.21 [ft]
C) 0.29 [ft]
D) 0.35 [ft]

Problem #32

Find: N ← the minimum number of staff needed to meet the work demand

Given:

all staff are scheduled to work for two consecutive 4-hour shifts, in a 24-hour time period.

staff can work the shift from 8:00 pm-4:00 am.

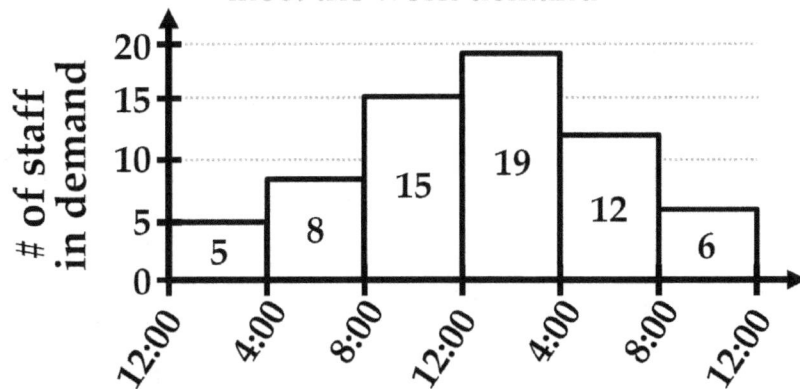

$w_i \geq d_i$

number of workers must meet or exceed the work demand for all 6 shifts

A) 32
B) 33
C) 34
D) 35

Problem #33

Find: Q_B ← the flow rate through pipe BE

Given:

$d = 6\,[\mathrm{in}]$
$L = 10\,[\mathrm{ft}]$
$f = 0.021$

the pipe diameter, length and friction coefficient for all 7 pipe segments in the network

$Q = 2.41\,[\mathrm{ft^3/s}]$ ← the total flow rate into and out of the system

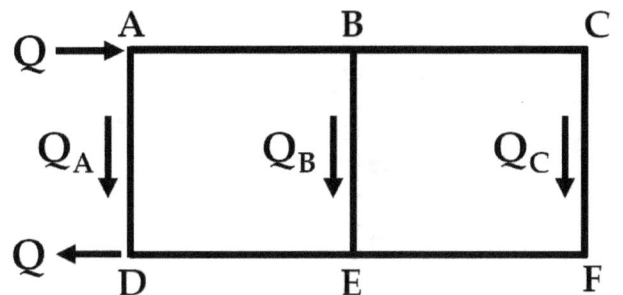

A) 0.346 [ft³/s]
B) 0.599 [ft³/s]
C) 1.011 [ft³/s]
D) 1.464 [ft³/s]

Civil Engineering Practice Examination #2

Problem #34

Find: η ← porosity of the soil sample

Given:

$SG = 2.70$ ← specific gravity of the solid material

$\varrho_T = 110 \ [\text{lb/ft}^3]$ ← total density of the soil sample

$S = 25\%$ ← saturation

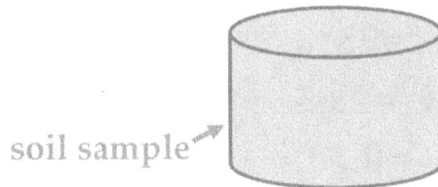

soil sample →

A) 0.16
B) 0.28
C) 0.38
D) 0.62

Problem #35

Find: G_1 ← the approach grade of the vertical curve

Given:

$STA_A = 3+50$
$Elev_A = 141.8 \ [\text{ft}]$

$STA_B = 4+50$
$Elev_B = 140.1 \ [\text{ft}]$

$STA_C = 6+00$
$Elev_C = 142.9 \ [\text{ft}]$

} the stationing and elevation of points A, B and C on the vertical curve

the vertical curve begins at point A

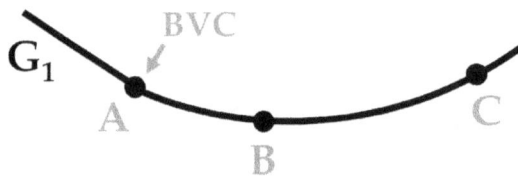

BVC

G_1

A

B

C

A) -1.1%
B) -2.1%
C) -3.1%
D) -4.1%

Problem #36

Find: $P(EF_C \leq 7)$ ← the probability the early finish of activity C is not later than week 7

Given: $ES_A = 1$ ← the early start of activity A

$D_A = 2$ ← the duration of activity A

project schedule →

Task	Pred
A	-
B	A
C	B

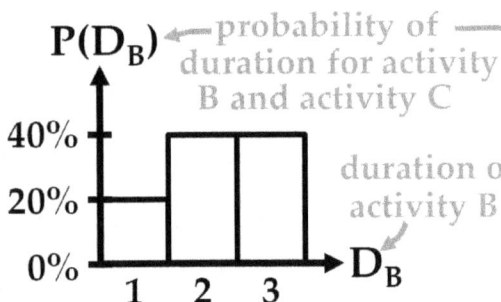

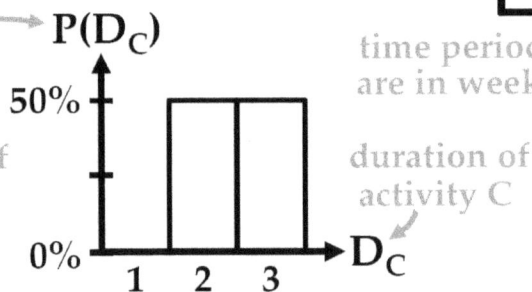

$P(D_B)$ ← probability of duration for activity B and activity C → $P(D_C)$

40%
20%
0%
1 2 3
D_B

duration of activity B

50%
0%
1 2 3
D_C

duration of activity C

time periods are in weeks

A) 10%
B) 20%
C) 40%
D) 60%

Problem #37

<u>Find:</u> v_c ← the critical velocity

<u>Given:</u> b=2[m] ← base width of the rectangular channel

C_2=0.590 ← coefficient for the triangular weir

H=1.4[m] ← total hydraulic head at the triangular weir

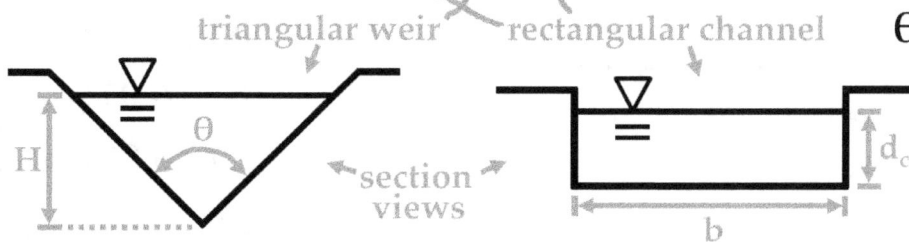

plan view of → channel and weir

Q →

triangular weir   rectangular channel

θ=90°

section views

H θ d_c

b

A) 0.52[m/s]
B) 1.04[m/s]
C) 1.63[m/s]
D) 2.51[m/s]

Problem #38

<u>Find:</u> C_U ← coefficient of uniformity

<u>Given:</u>

100%   #4 sieve

80%

Percent Passing (by mass)   60%

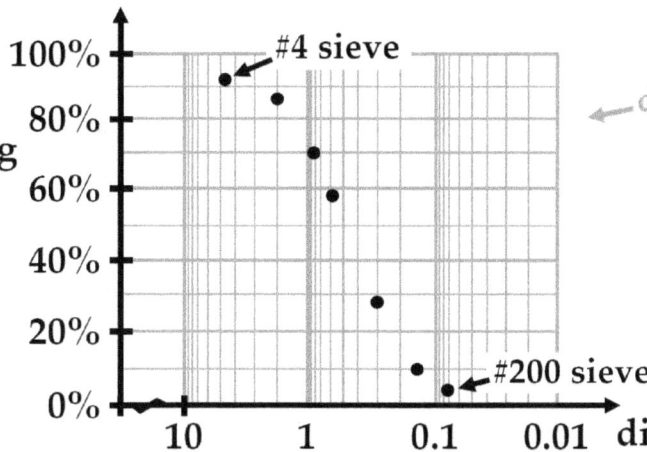

40%

20%

0%   #200 sieve

10   1   0.1   0.01   diameter [mm]

data from a sieve analysis test

A) 0.7
B) 1.7
C) 4.7
D) 9.8

Problem #39

<u>Find:</u> v_A ← the maximum vehicle velocity at point A which allows the driver to stop without hitting the object at point B.

<u>Given:</u>

R=40[m] ← radius of the horizontal curve

C_{AB}=70[m] ← chord length from point A to point B

a=3[m/s²]
↑
deceleration of the vehicle when breaking

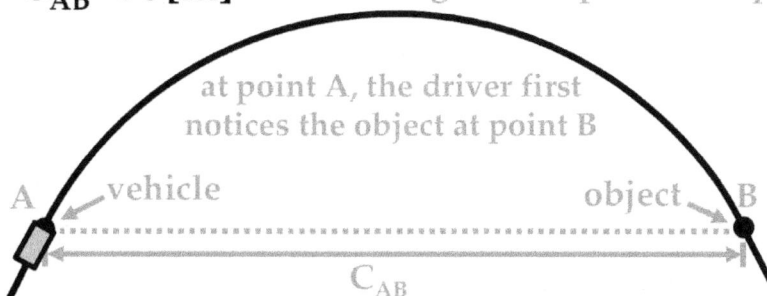

at point A, the driver first notices the object at point B

A   vehicle   object   B

C_{AB}

t_r=2.2[s]
reaction time of the driver

A) 17[km/hr]
B) 31[km/hr]
C) 47[km/hr]
D) 61[km/hr]

Civil Engineering Practice Examination #2

Problem #40

Find: d ← depth to the centroid of the area of steel

Given:

s = 1.5 [in] — vertical spacing between the two rows of reinforcing bars (edge to edge)

c = 2.0 [in] ← cover

w = 14 [in] ← beam width

h = 20 [in] ← beam height

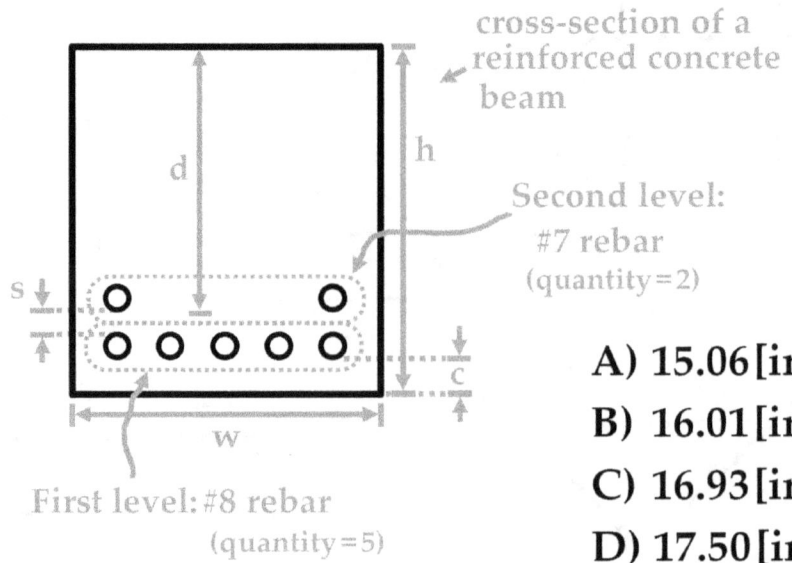

cross-section of a reinforced concrete beam

Second level: #7 rebar (quantity=2)

First level: #8 rebar (quantity=5)

A) 15.06 [in]

B) 16.01 [in]

C) 16.93 [in]

D) 17.50 [in]

Section 2: Detailed Solutions

(page intentionally left blank)

Solution #1

Find: A ← the total area of the roof

Given:

$\theta_A = 25°$　　$\theta_B = 15°$

the angle the roof makes with the horizon

$l_A = 25\,[\text{ft}]$
$l_B = 33\,[\text{ft}]$ the length of parts A and B

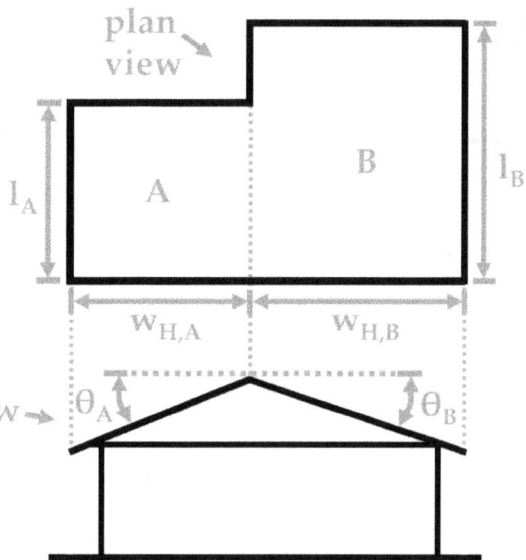

plan view

A　　B

l_A　　l_B

$w_{H,A}$　$w_{H,B}$

profile view →　θ_A　　θ_B

$w_{H,A} = 15\,[\text{ft}]$
$w_{H,B} = 20\,[\text{ft}]$

the horizontal width of part A and part B

A) $978\,[\text{ft}^2]$
B) $1,035\,[\text{ft}^2]$
C) $1,065\,[\text{ft}^2]$
D) $1,110\,[\text{ft}^2]$

Analysis:

total area $A = A_A + A_B$ ←eq.1

area of part A　　area of part B

Eq.1 computes the total area of the roof.

$A_A = l_A * w_A$ ←eq.2

length of part A　　width of part A.

Eq.2 computes the area of part A.

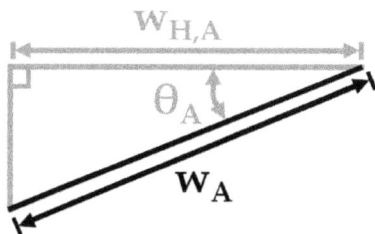

$w_{H,A}$

θ_A

w_A

Figure 1

Figure 1 shows the profile view of roof-line A with respect to the horizontal width of area A and angle θ_A.

$\cos(\theta_A) = \dfrac{w_{H,A}}{w_A}$ ←eq.3

width of roof A

Eq.3 computes the cosine of θ_A. Solve eq.3 for the width of roof area A, w_A.

$w_{H,A} = 15\,[\text{ft}]$

$w_A = \dfrac{w_{H,A}}{\cos(\theta_A)}$ ←eq.4

$\theta_A = 25°$

Plug in variables θ_A and $w_{H,A}$ into eq.4, then solve for w_A.

Solution #1 (cont.)

$$w_A = \frac{15\,[ft]}{\cos(25°)}$$

$$w_A = 16.55\,[ft]$$

$$A_A = l_A * w_A \leftarrow eq.2$$

$l_A = 25\,[ft]$ $w_A = 16.55\,[ft]$

Plug in variables l_A and w_A into eq.2, then solve for A_A.

$$A_A = 25\,[ft] * 16.55\,[ft]$$

$$A_A = 413.8\,[ft^2]$$

$$A_B = l_B * w_B \leftarrow eq.5$$

length of part B   width of part B.

Eq.5 computes the area of part B.

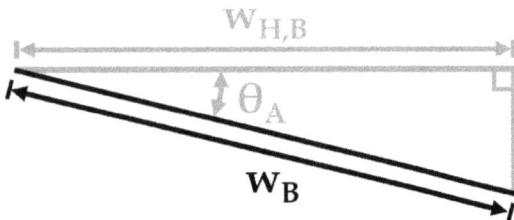

Figure 2

Figure 2 shows the profile view of roof-line B with respect to the horizontal width of area B and angle θ_B.

$$\cos(\theta_B) = \frac{w_{H,B}}{w_B} \leftarrow eq.6$$

width of roof B

$w_{H,B} = 20\,[ft]$

Eq.6 computes the cosine of θ_B. Solve eq.6 for the width of roof area B, w_B.

$$w_B = \frac{w_{H,B}}{\cos(\theta_B)} \leftarrow eq.7$$

$\theta_B = 15°$

Plug in variables θ_B and $w_{H,B}$ into eq.7, then solve for w_B.

$$w_B = \frac{20\,[ft]}{\cos(15°)}$$

$$w_B = 20.71\,[ft]$$

$$A_B = l_B * w_B \leftarrow eq.5$$

$$l_B = 33\,[ft] \qquad w_B = 20.71\,[ft]$$

Plug in variables l_B and w_B into eq.5, then solve for A_B.

$$A_B = 33\,[ft] * 20.71\,[ft]$$

$$A_B = 683.4\,[ft^2]$$

$$A = A_A + A_B \leftarrow eq.1$$

$$A_A = 413.8\,[ft^2] \qquad A_B = 683.4\,[ft^2]$$

Plug in variables A_A and A_B into eq.1, then solve for A.

$$A = 413.8\,[ft^2] + 683.4\,[ft^2]$$

$$A = 1{,}097\,[ft^2]$$

<u>Answer:</u> $\boxed{D}$

Civil Engineering Practice Examination #2

Solution #2

<u>Find:</u> Flow Classification

the channel side slopes are
1.5:1 (horizontal:vertical)

<u>Given:</u>

$Q=15\,[m^3/s]$ ←flow rate

$b=3\,[m]$ ←base width

$d=1\,[m]$ ←depth of flow

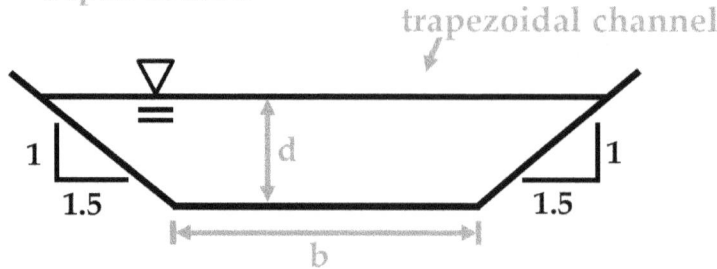

trapezoidal channel

A) supercritical

B) critical

C) subcritical

D) not enough information

Analysis:

If $Fr>1$ → supercritical

If $Fr=1$ → critical

If $Fr<1$ → subcritical

The flow classification depends on the Froude number, Fr.

Froude number   flow velocity

$$Fr= \frac{v}{\sqrt{g^*D_h}} \quad ←eq.1$$

gravitational acceleration   hydraulic depth

Eq. 1 computes the Froude number, as a function of the flow velocity, gravitational acceleration and the hydraulic depth.

Hydraulic depth is also referred to as the characteristic length.

cross-sectional area

$$D_h= \frac{A}{T} \quad ←eq.2$$

top width

Eq. 2 computes the hydraulic depth of the flow in the channel.

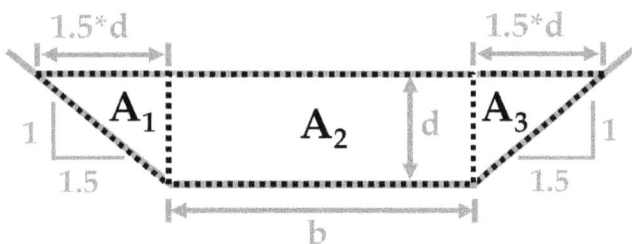

Figure 1 divides the cross-sectional area into 3 parts.

Figure 1

Solution #2 (cont.)

$$A = A_1 + A_2 + A_3 \leftarrow eq.3$$

Eq. 3 computes the area of the flow as the sum of the three sub areas identified in Figure 1.

$$A_1 = A_3 = 0.5 * d * 1.5 * d \leftarrow eq.4$$
$$d = 1 [m]$$

Eq. 4 computes sub areas 1 and 3, based on the depth of flow.

$$A_1 = A_3 = 0.5 * 1 [m] * 1.5 * 1 [m]$$

Plug in the depth, d, into eq. 4, then solve for sub areas 1 and 3.

$$A_1 = A_3 = 0.75 [m^2]$$

$$A_2 = b * d \leftarrow eq.5$$
$$b = 3 [m] \quad d = 1 [m]$$

Eq. 5 computes sub area 2.

$$A_2 = 3 [m] * 1 [m]$$

$$A_2 = 3 [m^2]$$

$$A_1 = A_3 = 0.75 [m^2]$$
$$A = A_1 + A_2 + A_3 \leftarrow eq.3$$
$$A_2 = 3 [m^2]$$

Plug in variables A_1, A_2 and A_3 into 3, then solve for A.

$$A = 0.75 [m^2] + 3 [m^2] + 0.75 [m^2]$$

$$A = 4.50 [m^2]$$

$$b = 3 [m] \quad d = 1 [m]$$
$$T = 1.5 * d + b + 1.5 * d \leftarrow eq.6$$
$$\text{side slope}$$

Eq. 6 computes the top width of flow based on the base width, the water depth, and the side slope.

$$T = 1.5 * 1 [m] + 3 [m] + 1.5 * 1 [m]$$

Solution #2 (cont.)

$$T = 6 \, [\text{m}]$$

$$A = 4.50 \, [\text{m}^2]$$
$$\downarrow$$
$$D_h = \frac{A}{T} \leftarrow eq.2$$
$$\uparrow$$
$$T = 6 \, [\text{m}]$$

Plug in variables A and T into eq.2, then solve for D_h.

$$D_h = \frac{4.50 \, [\text{m}^2]}{6 \, [\text{m}]}$$

$$D_h = 0.75 \, [\text{m}]$$

$$Q = 15 \, [\text{m}^3/\text{s}]$$
$$\searom$$
$$v = \frac{Q}{A} \leftarrow eq.7$$
$$A = 4.50 \, [\text{m}^2]$$

Eq.7 computes the velocity of flow as the flow rate divided by the cross-sectional area.

Plug in variables Q and A into eq.7, then solve for v.

$$v = \frac{15 \, [\text{m}^3/\text{s}]}{4.50 \, [\text{m}^2]}$$

$$v = 3.33 \, [\text{m/s}]$$

$$v = 3.33 \, [\text{m/s}]$$
$$\downarrow$$
$$Fr = \frac{v}{\sqrt{g * D_h}} \leftarrow eq.1$$
$$g = 9.81 \, [\text{m/s}^2] \quad D_h = 0.75 \, [\text{m}]$$

Plug in variables v, g and D_h into eq.1, then solve for Fr.

Since the Froude number is greater than 1, the flow classification is "supercritical"

$$Fr = \frac{3.33 \, [\text{m/s}]}{\sqrt{9.81 \, [\text{m/s}^2] * 0.75 \, [\text{m}]}}$$

$$Fr = 1.23 \qquad Fr > 1 \longrightarrow \text{supercritical} \qquad \underline{\text{Answer:}} \quad \boxed{A}$$

Solution #3

<u>Find:</u> **S** ← saturation of the soil sample

<u>Given:</u>

SG = 2.69 ← specific gravity of the solid material

V_T = 1 [cm³] ← total volume

e = 0.70 ← void ratio

wc = 12% ← water content

] ← properties of the soil sample

soil sample →

A) 12%
B) 19%
C) 41%
D) 46%

Analysis:

volume of water

$$S = \frac{V_W}{V_V} \leftarrow eq.1$$

saturation ↗ ↘ volume of voids

Eq.1 calculates the saturation of the soil sample.

$$V_V = V_A + V_W \leftarrow eq.2$$

volume of air

Eq.2 calculates the volume of voids as the sum of the volume of air and water.

mass of water

$$V_W = M_W / \varrho_W \leftarrow eq.3$$

water density

Eq.3 calculates the volume of water as the mass of water divided by the density of water.

$$V_T = V_S * (1+e) \leftarrow eq.4$$

volume of solid material ↗ ↖ void ratio

Eq.4 calculates the total volume of the soil sample.

Solve eq.4 for V_S.

$$V_S = V_T / (1+e) \leftarrow eq.5$$

$V_T = 1 [cm³]$ e = 0.70

Plug in variables V_T and e into eq.5, then solve for V_S.

$$V_S = 1 [cm³] / (1+0.70)$$

Solution #3 (cont.)

$$V_S = 0.588\,[\text{cm}^3]$$

Eq.6 computes the mass of the solid material in the sample based on the volume of solid material and the density of the solid material.

$$\underset{\underset{\text{SG}=2.69}{\nwarrow}\;\;\underset{\varrho_W=1\,[\text{g/cm}^3]}{\uparrow}}{\overset{V_S=0.588\,[\text{cm}^3]}{\downarrow}}{M_S = V_S * SG * \varrho_W} \leftarrow eq.6$$

Plug in variables V_S, SG and ϱ_W into eq.6, then solve for M_S.

$$M_S = 0.588\,[\text{cm}^3] * 2.69 * 1\,[\text{g/cm}^3]$$

$$M_S = 1.582\,[\text{g}]$$

Eq.7 computes the water content as the mass of water divided by the mass of solid.

$$wc = \frac{M_W}{M_S} \leftarrow eq.7$$

Solve eq. 7 for M_W.

$$\underset{\underset{wc=12\%=0.12}{\nearrow}\;\;\underset{M_S=1.582\,[\text{g}]}{\uparrow}}{M_W = wc * M_S} \leftarrow eq.8$$

Plug in variables wc and M_S into eq.8, then solve for M_W.

$$M_W = 0.12 * 1.582\,[\text{g}]$$

$$M_W = 0.190\,[\text{g}]$$

$$\underset{\underset{\varrho_W=1\,[\text{g/cm}^3]}{\uparrow}}{\overset{M_W=0.190\,[\text{g}]}{\downarrow}}{V_W = M_W / \varrho_W} \leftarrow eq.3$$

Plug in variables M_W and ϱ_W into eq.3, then solve for V_W.

$$V_W = 0.190\,[\text{g}] / 1\,[\text{g/cm}^3]$$

$$V_W = 0.190\,[\text{cm}^3]$$

$$V_T = V_A + V_S + V_W \leftarrow eq.9$$

Eq. 9 computes the total volume of the soil sample.

Solution #3 (cont.)

$V_S = 0.588\,[cm^3]$

$$V_A = V_T - V_S - V_W \leftarrow eq.10$$

$V_T = 1\,[cm^3] \qquad V_W = 0.190\,[cm^3]$

Solve eq. 9 for variable V_A.

Plug in variables V_T, V_S and V_W into eq.10, then solve for V_A.

$$V_A = 1\,[cm^3] - 0.588\,[cm^3] - 0.190\,[cm^3]$$

$$V_A = 0.222\,[cm^3]$$

$$V_V = V_A + V_W \leftarrow eq.2$$

$V_A = 0.222\,[cm^3] \qquad V_W = 0.190\,[cm^3]$

Plug in variables V_A and V_W into eq.2, then solve for V_V.

$$V_V = 0.222\,[cm^3] + 0.190\,[cm^3]$$

$$V_V = 0.412\,[cm^3]$$

$V_W = 0.190\,[cm^3]$

$$S = \frac{V_W}{V_V} \leftarrow eq.1$$

$V_V = 0.412\,[cm^3]$

Plug in variables V_W and V_V into eq.1, then solve for S.

$$S = \frac{0.190\,[cm^3]}{0.412\,[cm^3]}$$

$$S = 0.461$$

$$S = 46.1\%$$

Answer: $\boxed{D}$

Solution #4

Find: I ← the interior angle of the curve

Given:

$L_{AB} = 150\,[m]$ ← the length along the larger curve

$L_{XC} = 123\,[m]$ ← the radius of the the smaller curve

$2*L_{XC} = L_{YB}$

the two horizontal curves have the same interior angle

A) 30°
B) 35°
C) 40°
D) 45°

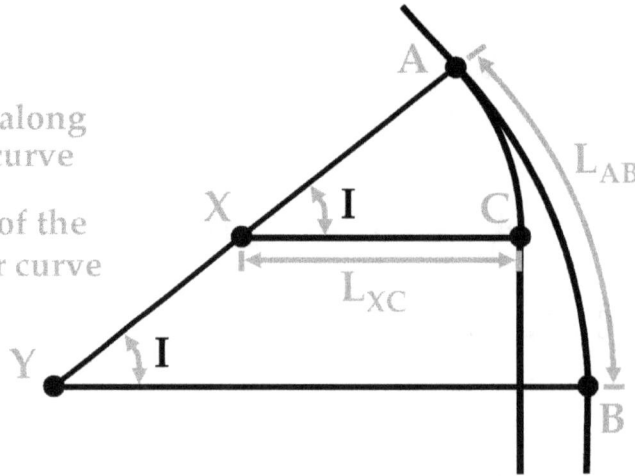

Analysis:

$L = L_{AC}$ → curve length

$$I = \frac{360°*L}{2*\pi*R} \leftarrow eq.1$$

$R = L_{XC}$ ← curve radius

Eq. 1 computes the interior angle of a horizontal curve.

$$I = \frac{360°*L_{AC}}{2*\pi*L_{XC}} \leftarrow eq.2$$

Substitute in the curve length and curve radius into eq. 1, for the smaller horizontal curve.

$$2*L_{XC} = L_{YB} \leftarrow eq.3$$

Eq. 3 states the radius of the larger curve is twice the radius of the shorter curve.

$$L_{XC} = 0.5*L_{YB} \leftarrow eq.4$$

Solve eq. 3 for L_{XC}.

$$I_{AYB} = I_{AXC} \leftarrow eq.5$$

Eq. 5 shows that the two horizontal angles share the same interior angle.

$$I_{AYB} = \frac{360°*L_{AB}}{2*\pi*L_{YB}} \qquad I_{AXC} = \frac{360°*L_{AC}}{2*\pi*L_{XC}}$$

Plug in the known equations for the interior angles into eq. 5.

$$\frac{360°*L_{AB}}{2*\pi*L_{YB}} = \frac{360°*L_{AC}}{2*\pi*L_{XC}} \leftarrow eq.6$$

Cancel out the equivalent terms appearing on both sides of eq. 6.

Solution #4 (cont.)

$L_{AB} = 150\,[m]$

$$\frac{L_{AB}}{L_{YB}} = \frac{L_{AC}}{L_{XC}} \leftarrow eq.\,7$$

$L_{XC} = 0.5 * L_{YB}$

Plug in variables L_{AB} and L_{XC} into eq. 7, then solve for L_{AC}.

$$\frac{150\,[m]}{L_{YB}} = \frac{L_{AC}}{0.5 * L_{YB}}$$

$$L_{AC} = 75\,[m]$$

$L_{AC} = 75\,[m]$

$$I = \frac{360° * L_{AC}}{2 * \pi * L_{XC}} \leftarrow eq.\,2$$

$L_{XC} = 123\,[m]$

Plug in variables L_{AC} and L_{XC} into eq. 2 then solve for I.

$$I = \frac{360° * 75\,[m]}{2 * \pi * 123\,[m]}$$

$$I = 34.9°$$

Answer: $\boxed{\text{B}}$

Civil Engineering Practice Examination #2

Solution #5

Find: $y_{(x=L)}$ ← the vertical deflection at the end of the cantilever beam

Given:

$L_1 = 6\,[\text{ft}]$ ⎱ length along the beam
$L_2 = 6\,[\text{ft}]$ ⎰

$w = 7\,[\text{k/ft}]$ ← uniform load along length L_2 of the beam.

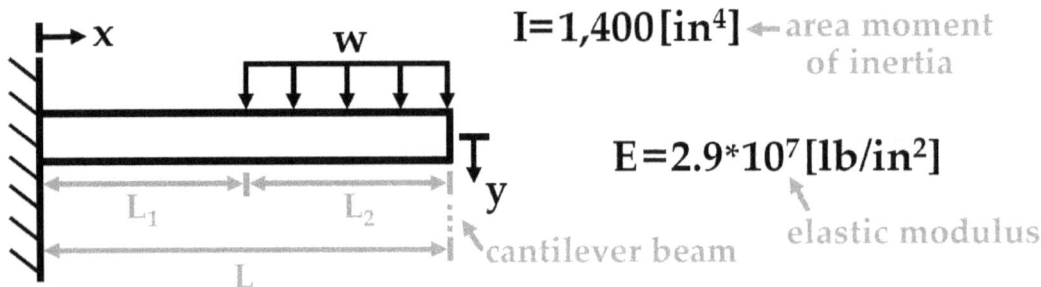

$I = 1,400\,[\text{in}^4]$ ← area moment of inertia

$E = 2.9 * 10^7\,[\text{lb/in}^2]$ ← elastic modulus

cantilever beam

A) 0.11 [in]
B) 0.66 [in]
C) 0.77 [in]
D) 0.88 [in]

Analysis:

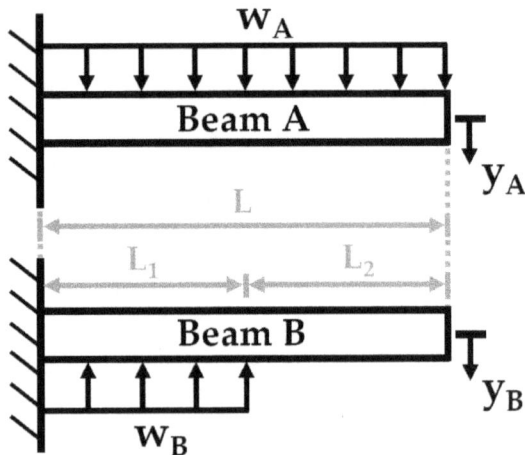

Figure 1

Figure 1 shows uniformly loaded cantilever Beams A and B.

Assume Beam A and Beam B have the same length, elastic modulus and area moment of inertia values as defined in the problem statement.

Use the principle of superposition.

$$y_{(x=L)} = y_{A(x=L)} + y_{B(x=L)} \quad \leftarrow eq.1$$

the deflection at the end of Beam A and Beam B

Eq. 1 computes the deflection at the end of the beam.

uniform load ↘ ↙ beam length

$$y_{A(x=L)} = \frac{w_A * L^4}{8 * E * I} \quad \leftarrow eq.2$$

elastic modulus ↗ ↖ area moment of inertia

Eq. 2 computes the deflection at the end of Beam A.

$$w_A = w = 7\,[\text{k/ft}] * 1,000 \left[\frac{\text{lb}}{\text{k}}\right] \quad \leftarrow eq.3$$

Eq. 3 converts the uniform load of Beam A to pounds per foot.

Solution #5 (cont.)

$$w_A = 7,000 \, [\text{lb/ft}]$$

$$L = L_1 + L_2 \leftarrow eq.4$$

$$L_1 = 6 \, [\text{ft}] \qquad L_2 = 6 \, [\text{ft}]$$

Eq.4 computes the total length of the beam.

$$L = 6 \, [\text{ft}] + 6 \, [\text{ft}]$$

Plug in variables L_1 and L_2 into eq.4, then solve for L.

$$L = 12 \, [\text{ft}]$$

$$w_A = 7,000 \, [\text{lb/ft}] \qquad L = 12 \, [\text{ft}]$$

$$y_{A(x=L)} = \frac{w_A * L^4}{8 * E * I} \leftarrow eq.2$$

$$E = 2.9*10^7 \, [\text{lb/in}^2] \qquad I = 1,400 \, [\text{in}^4]$$

Plug in variables w_A, L, E and I into eq.2, then solve for $y_{A(x=L)}$.

$$y_{A(x=L)} = \frac{7,000 \, [\text{lb/ft}] * (12 \, [\text{ft}])^4}{8 * 2.9*10^7 \, [\text{lb/in}^2] * 1,400 \, [\text{in}^4]}$$

$$y_{A(x=L)} = 4.469 * 10^{-4} \left[\frac{\text{ft}^3}{\text{in}^2}\right] * \left(12 \left[\frac{\text{in}}{\text{ft}}\right]\right)^3$$

Convert the deflection in Beam A to inches.

$$y_{A(x=L)} = 0.772 \, [\text{in}]$$

uniform load

$$y_{B(x=L)} = \frac{w_B * L_1^4}{8 * E * I} + L_2 * \frac{w_B * L_1^3}{6 * E * I} \leftarrow eq.5$$

elastic modulus   area moment of inertia

Eq.5 computes the deflection at the end of the beam caused by uniform load w_B.

$$w_B = -w = -7,000 \, [\text{lb/ft}]$$

Set the uniform load of Beam B as a negative value because it causes an upward deflection in the beam.

Civil Engineering Practice Examination #2

Solution #5 (cont.)

Plug in variables w_B, L_1, L_2, E and I into eq.5, then solve for $y_{B(x=L)}$.

$w_B = -7,000\,[\text{lb/ft}]$ $L_1 = 6\,[\text{ft}]$

$E = 2.9 * 10^7\,[\text{lb/in}^2]$ $I = 1,400\,[\text{in}^4]$

$L_2 = 6\,[\text{ft}]$

$$y_{B(x=L)} = \frac{w_B * L_1^4}{8 * E * I} + L_2 * \frac{w_B * L_1^3}{6 * E * I} \leftarrow eq.5$$

$$y_{B(x=L)} = \frac{(-7,000\,[\text{lb/ft}]) * (6\,[\text{ft}])^4}{8 * 2.9*10^7\,[\text{lb/in}^2] * 1,400\,[\text{in}^4]} + 6\,[\text{ft}] * \frac{(-7,000\,[\text{lb/ft}]) * (6\,[\text{ft}])^3}{6 * 2.9*10^7\,[\text{lb/in}^2] * 1,400\,[\text{in}^4]}$$

$$y_{B(x=L)} = -6.514 * 10^{-5}\left[\frac{\text{ft}^3}{\text{in}^2}\right] * \left(12\left[\frac{\text{in}}{\text{ft}}\right]\right)^3$$

Convert the deflection in Beam B to inches.

$$y_{B(x=L)} = -0.113\,[\text{in}]$$

$y_{A(x=L)} = 0.772\,[\text{in}]$ $y_{B(x=L)} = -0.113\,[\text{in}]$

$$y_{(x=L)} = y_{A(x=L)} + y_{B(x=L)} \leftarrow eq.1$$

Plug in variables $y_{A(x=L)}$ and $y_{B(x=L)}$ into eq.1, then solve for $y_{(x=L)}$.

$$y_{(x=L)} = 0.772\,[\text{in}] + (-0.113\,[\text{in}])$$

$$y_{(x=L)} = 0.659\,[\text{in}]$$

Answer: $\boxed{\text{B}}$

Solution #6

Find: q_{ult} ← ultimate bearing capacity of the square footing

Given:

$d = 0 \, [ft]$ ← depth of footing beneath soil surface

$\phi = 20°$ ← friction angle

$c = 0 \, [lb/ft^2]$ ← cohesion

$\gamma = 115 \, [lb/ft^3]$ ← unit weight

load

no groundwater table

$B = W = 8 \, [ft]$

base length and width of the square footing

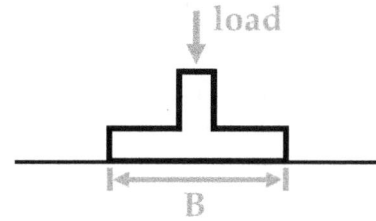

A) $1{,}000 \, [lb/ft^2]$

B) $2{,}000 \, [lb/ft^2]$

C) $3{,}000 \, [lb/ft^2]$

D) $4{,}000 \, [lb/ft^2]$

Analysis:

bearing capacity factors

Eq. 1 computes the ultimate bearing capacity of a square footing.

$$q_{ult} = 1.2 * c * N_c + 0.4 * \gamma * B * N_\gamma + q * N_q \leftarrow eq.1$$

cohesion   effective unit weight   footing width   effective stress

Eq. 2 computes the effective stress at the base of the footing.

$$q = d * \gamma' \leftarrow eq.2$$

$d = 0 \, [ft]$ $\gamma' = \gamma = 115 \, [lb/ft^3]$

Since there is no groundwater table, the effective unit weight equals the total unit weight of the soil.

$$q = 0 \, [ft] * 115 \, [lb/ft^3]$$

$$q = 0 \, [lb/ft^2]$$

Plug in variables d and γ' into eq. 2, then solve for q.

$$N_q = \tan^2(45° + \phi/2) * e^{\pi * \tan(\phi)} \leftarrow eq.3$$

$\phi = 20°$

Eq. 3 computes the bearing capacity factor N_q.

Plug in ϕ into eq. 3, then solve for N_q.

$$N_q = \tan^2(45° + 20°/2) * e^{\pi * \tan(20°)}$$

$$N_q = 6.402$$

Eq. 4 computes the bearing capacity factor N_γ.

$$N_\gamma = 2 * (N_q + 1) * \tan(\phi) \leftarrow eq.4$$

$N_q = 6.402$ $\phi = 20°$

Plug in N_q and ϕ into eq. 4, then solve for N_γ.

Solution #6 (cont.)

$$N_\gamma = 2*(6.402+1)*\tan(20°)$$

$$N_\gamma = 5.388$$

Plug in variables c, γ, B, N_γ and q into eq.1, then solve for q_{ult}.

$c = 0 \, [lb/ft^2]$ $B = 8 \, [ft]$ $q = 0 \, [lb/ft^2]$

$$q_{ult} = 1.2*c*N_c + 0.4*\gamma*B*N_\gamma + q*N_q \leftarrow eq.1$$

$\gamma = 115 \, [lb/ft^3]$ $N_\gamma = 5.388$

$$q_{ult} = 1.2*0\,[lb/ft^2]*N_c + 0.4*115\,[lb/ft^3]*8\,[ft]*5.388 + 0\,[lb/ft^2]*N_q$$

$$q_{ult} = 1,982 \, [lb/ft^2]$$

Answer: $\boxed{\text{B}}$

Detailed Solutions

Solution #7

<u>Find</u>: P_B ← the pressure at point B

<u>Given</u>: $Q = 0.20 [ft^3/s]$ ← flow rate

$L = 60 [ft]$ ← pipe length

$P_A = 80 [lb_f/in^2]$ ← pressure at point A

$C = 100$ ← Hazen-Williams roughness coefficient

$k_{valve} = 2.3$ ⎫ minor headloss coefficients for
$k_{90°} = 0.9$ ⎭ a check valve and 90° elbow

$d = 4 [in]$ ← pipe diameter

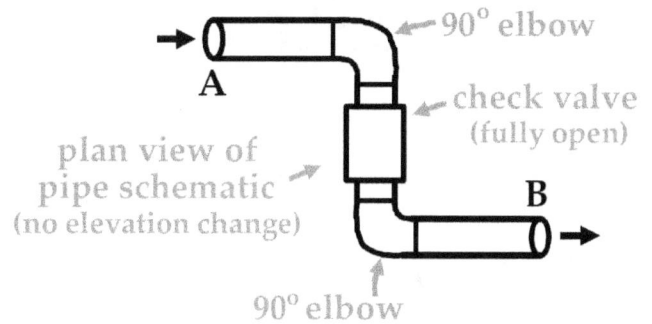

plan view of pipe schematic (no elevation change)

→ A

← 90° elbow

← check valve (fully open)

B

90° elbow

water

fluid flowing through the pipe

A) $75.2 [lb_f/in^2]$
B) $76.7 [lb_f/in^2]$
C) $78.1 [lb_f/in^2]$
D) $79.6 [lb_f/in^2]$

Analysis:

energy at point A

change in energy from point A to point B

$$E_A = E_B + \Delta E_{AB} \leftarrow eq.1$$

energy at point B

Eq.1 relates the total energy of the pipe flow at points A and B.

headloss

$$\boxed{\frac{P_A}{\gamma_A}} + \boxed{\frac{v_A^2}{2*g}} + z_A = \boxed{\frac{P_B}{\gamma_B}} + \boxed{\frac{v_B^2}{2*g}} + z_B + \Delta h_{AB} \leftarrow eq.2$$

pressure head

velocity head

elevation head

Eq.2 is Bernoulli's equation showing the total energy at points A and B are divided into pressure head, velocity head and elevation head.

$$P_B = \gamma_B * \left(\frac{P_A}{\gamma_A} + \frac{v_A^2}{2*g} + z_A - \frac{v_B^2}{2*g} - z_B - \Delta h_{AB} \right) \leftarrow eq.3$$

$\gamma_B = \gamma_A$

Solve eq.2 for the pressure at point B.

Since the unit weight of water, the velocity and the elevation are the same at points A and B, we can cancel velocity head terms and elevation head terms from eq.3, and simplify.

pressure at points B and A

$$P_B = P_A - \gamma_w * \Delta h_{AB} \leftarrow eq.4$$

unit weight of water

headloss between point A and point B

$$\Delta h_{AB} = \boxed{\frac{10.44 * L * Q^{1.85}}{C^{1.85} * d^{4.87}}} + \boxed{\Sigma \left(k * \frac{v^2}{2*g} \right)} \leftarrow eq.5$$

major headloss

minor headloss

Eq.5 computes the headloss between points A and B by adding the major headloss to the minor headloss.

35

Civil Engineering Practice Examination #2

Solution #7 (cont.)

The major headloss term in eq. 5 requires the flow rate to be in gallons per minute.

$$Q = 0.20 \left[\frac{ft^3}{s}\right] * 7.48 \left[\frac{gal}{ft^3}\right] * 60 \left[\frac{s}{min}\right] \leftarrow eq. 6$$

Eq. 6 converts the flow to units of gallons per minute.

$$Q = 89.76 \, [gal/min]$$

velocity   minor headloss coefficients

$$\Sigma\left(k * \frac{v^2}{2*g}\right) = \left(\frac{v^2}{2*g}\right) * \Sigma k \leftarrow eq. 7$$

gravitational acceleration

Eq. 7 computes the minor headloss in the pipe.

flow rate

$$v = \frac{Q}{A} \leftarrow eq. 8$$

cross-sectional area of the pipe

Eq. 8 computes the velocity of the water flowing through the pipe.

$d = 4 \, [in]$

$$A = \frac{\pi * d^2}{4} \leftarrow eq. 9$$

Eq. 9 computes the area of the pipe based on the pipe diameter.

$$A = \frac{\pi * (4 \, [in])^2}{4}$$

Plug in variable d into eq. 9, then solve for the area, A.

$$A = 12.57 \, [in^2] * \left(\frac{1}{12}\left[\frac{ft}{in}\right]\right)^2 \leftarrow eq. 10$$

Eq. 10 converts the area of the pipe to units of feet squared.

$$A = 0.0873 \, [ft^2]$$

$Q = 0.20 \, [ft^3/s]$

$$v = \frac{Q}{A} \leftarrow eq. 8$$

$A = 0.0873 \, [ft^2]$

Plug in variables Q and A into eq. 8, then solve for v.

$$v = \frac{0.20 \, [ft^3/s]}{0.0873 \, [ft^2]}$$

$$v = 2.291 \, [ft/s]$$

$k_{90°}=0.9$ $k_{valve}=2.3$

$$\Sigma k = 2 * k_{90°} + k_{valve} \quad \leftarrow eq.\,11$$

Eq. 11 sums up the minor headloss coefficients.

$$\Sigma k = 2 * 0.9 + 2.3$$

$$\Sigma k = 4.1$$

$v=2.291\,[ft/s]$

$\Sigma k = 4.1$

$$\Sigma \left(k * \frac{v^2}{2*g} \right) = \left(\frac{v^2}{2*g} \right) * \Sigma k \quad \leftarrow eq.\,7$$

$32.2\,[ft/s^2]$

Plug in variables v, g and Σk into eq. 7, then solve for the minor headloss.

$$\Sigma \left(k * \frac{v^2}{2*g} \right) = \left(\frac{(2.291\,[ft/s])^2}{2*32.2[ft/s^2]} \right) * 4.1$$

$$\Sigma \left(k * \frac{v^2}{2*g} \right) = 0.33\,[ft]$$

Plug in variables L, Q, C, d and the minor headloss into eq. 5, then compute the total headloss between points A and B.

$L=60\,[ft]$ $Q=89.76\,[gal/min]$

$$\Delta h_{AB} = \frac{10.44 * L * Q^{1.85}}{C^{1.85} * d^{4.87}} + \Sigma \left(k * \frac{v^2}{2*g} \right) \quad \leftarrow eq.\,5$$

$C=100$ $d=4[in]$ $\Sigma \left(k * \frac{v^2}{2*g} \right) = 0.33\,[ft]$

Drop the units of flow and diameter in the major headloss term.

$$\Delta h_{AB} = \frac{10.44 * 60\,[ft] * (89.76)^{1.85}}{(100)^{1.85} * (4)^{4.87}} + 0.33\,[ft]$$

$$\Delta h_{AB} = 0.93\,[ft]$$

Eq. 12 computes the unit weight of water by multiplying by the density of water by gravitational acceleration constant and dividing by the gravitational conversion constant.

$\sigma_w = 62.4\,[lb_m/ft^3]$ $g=32.2\,[ft/s^3]$

$$\gamma_w = \sigma_w * \frac{g}{g_c} \quad \leftarrow eq.\,12$$

$g_c = 32.2 \left[\dfrac{lb_m * ft}{lb_f * s^2} \right]$

Solution #7 (cont.)

$$\gamma_w = 62.4 \left[\frac{\text{lb}_m}{\text{ft}^3}\right] * \frac{32.2\,[\text{ft/s}^2]}{32.2\,\left[\frac{\text{lb}_m * \text{ft}}{\text{lb}_f * \text{s}^2}\right]}$$

$$\gamma_w = 62.4 \left[\frac{\text{lb}_f}{\text{ft}^3}\right] * \left(\frac{1}{12}\left[\frac{\text{ft}}{\text{in}}\right]\right)^2$$

Convert the unit weight to pounds per inches squared per foot by dividing by a conversion factor.

conversion factor

$$\gamma_w = 0.433 \left[\frac{\text{lb}_f}{\text{ft} * \text{in}^2}\right]$$

$$\gamma_w = 0.433 \left[\frac{\text{lb}_f}{\text{ft} * \text{in}^2}\right]$$

Plug in variables P_A, g_w and Δh_{AB} into eq. 4, then solve for P_B.

$$P_B = P_A - \gamma_w * \Delta h_{AB} \leftarrow eq.\,4$$

$$P_A = 80\,[\text{lb}_f/\text{in}^2] \qquad \Delta h_{AB} = 0.93\,[\text{ft}]$$

$$P_B = 80\,[\text{lb}_f/\text{in}^2] - 0.433 \left[\frac{\text{lb}_f}{\text{ft} * \text{in}^2}\right] * 0.93\,[\text{ft}]$$

$$P_B = 79.60\,[\text{lb}_f/\text{in}^2]$$

<u>Answer:</u> $\boxed{\text{D}}$

Solution #8

Find: A ← area of coating on a single pile

Given:

$Elev_{HSL}=125.7\,[ft]$ ← high sea level

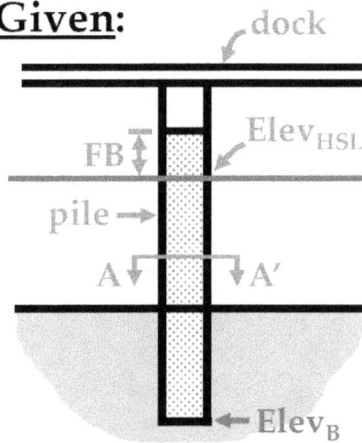

coating covers the entire pile up to the high sea level elevation plus the freeboard height, and base

$Elev_B=86.4\,[ft]$ ← elevation at pile base

$FB=4\,[ft]$ ← freeboard

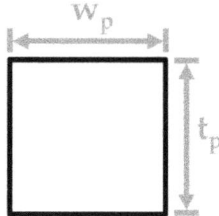

$w_p=2.5\,[ft]$ ← pile width

$t_p=2.5\,[ft]$ ← pile thickness

dock

FB

$Elev_{HSL}$

pile →

A ↓   ↓A′

← $Elev_B$

w_p

t_p

Section A-A′

A) $245\,[ft^2]$
B) $271\,[ft^2]$
C) $433\,[ft^2]$
D) $439\,[ft^2]$

Analysis:

total area of coating

area of coating on the "width side" of the pile

$$A=A_B+2*A_w+2*A_t \leftarrow eq.1$$

area of pile the base

area of coating on the "thickness side" of the pile

Eq. 1 calculates the total area of coating on a single pile.

$$A_B=t_p*w_p \leftarrow eq.2$$

$t_p=2.5\,[ft]$ $w_p=2.5\,[ft]$

Eq. 2 computes the base area of the pile.

$$A_B=2.5\,[ft]*2.5\,[ft]$$

Plug in the given pile width and thickness into eq. 2, then solve for the base area of the pile.

$$A_B=6.25\,[ft^2]$$

Eq. 3 computes the area of coating on the "width side" of the pile.

$Elev_{HSL}=125.7\,[ft]$ $FB=4\,[ft]$

$$A_w=w_p*(Elev_{HSL}+FB-Elev_B) \leftarrow eq.3$$

$w_p=2.5\,[ft]$ $Elev_B=86.4\,[ft]$

Plug in variables w_p, $Elev_{HSL}$, FB and $Elev_B$ into eq.3, then solve for A_w.

$$A_w=2.5\,[ft]*(125.7\,[ft]+4\,[ft]-86.4\,[ft])$$

$$A_w=108.25\,[ft^2]$$

Solution #8 (cont.)

Eq. 4 computes the area of coating on the "thickness side" of the pile.

$Elev_{HSL}=125.7\,[ft]$ $FB=4\,[ft]$

$$A_t = t_p * (Elev_{HSL} + FB - Elev_B) \leftarrow eq.4$$

$t_p = 2.5\,[ft]$ $Elev_B = 86.4\,[ft]$

Plug in variables t_p, $Elev_{HSL}$, FB and $Elev_B$ into eq.4, then solve for A_t.

$$A_t = 2.5\,[ft] * (125.7\,[ft] + 4\,[ft] - 86.4\,[ft])$$

$$A_t = 108.25\,[ft^2]$$

$A_w = 108.25\,[ft^2]$

$$A = A_B + 2*A_w + 2*A_t \leftarrow eq.1$$

$A_B = 6.25\,[ft^2]$ $A_t = 108.25\,[ft^2]$

Plug in variables A_B, A_w and A_t into eq.1, then solve for the area of coating on a single pile.

$$A = 6.25\,[ft^2] + 2*108.25\,[ft^2] + 2*108.25\,[ft^2]$$

$$A = 439.25\,[ft^2]$$

Answer: $\boxed{D}$

Solution #9

<u>Find:</u> **SRR** ← the superelevation runoff rate

<u>Given:</u>

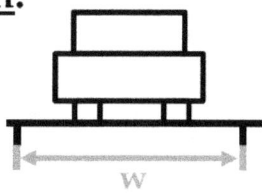

STA$_A$=150[m]

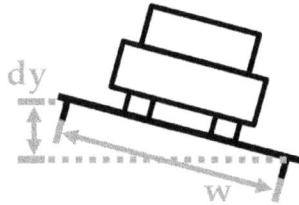

STA$_B$=216[m]

w=3.8[m]
↑ lane width

A) 1/180

B) 1/200

C) 1/220

D) 1/240

R=80[m] ← radius of the horizontal curve

dy=0.33[m] ← the superelevation at station B

<u>Analysis:</u>

width   superelevation rate

$$L = \frac{w * e}{SRR} \leftarrow eq.1$$

superelevation runoff

superelevation runoff rate

Eq.1 computes the superelevation runoff.

$$SRR = \frac{w * e}{L} \leftarrow eq.2$$

Solve eq.1 for the super-elevation runoff rate.

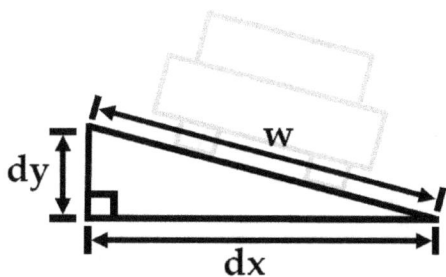

Figure 1

Figure 1 highlights the slope of the road at Station B.

$$e = dy/dx \leftarrow eq.3$$

Eq.3 computes the superelevation rate.

$$dx = \sqrt{w^2 - dy^2} \leftarrow eq.4$$

w=3.8[m]   dy=0.33[m]

Eq.4 computes the horizontal distance of the lane at station B.

Plug in variables w and dy into eq.4, then solve for dx.

Solution #9 (cont.)

$$dx = \sqrt{(3.8\,[m])^2 - (0.33\,[m])^2}$$

$$dx = 3.786\,[m]$$

$$e = dy/dx \leftarrow eq.3$$

$dy = 0.33\,[m] \qquad dx = 3.786\,[m]$

$$e = 0.33\,[m]/3.786\,[m]$$

$$e = 0.0872$$

$$L = STA_B - STA_A \leftarrow eq.5$$

$STA_B = 216\,[m] \qquad STA_A = 150\,[m]$

Eq. 5 computes the length between Station A and Station B.

Plug in variables STA_A and STA_B, then solve for L.

$$L = 216\,[m] - 150\,[m]$$

$$L = 66\,[m]$$

$w = 3.8\,[m] \qquad e = 0.0872$

$$SRR = \frac{w * e}{L} \leftarrow eq.2$$

$L = 66\,[m]$

Solve eq. 1 for the super-elevation runoff rate.

$$SRR = \frac{3.8\,[m] * 0.0872}{66\,[m]}$$

$$SRR = 0.00502$$

$$SRR = 1/199.2 \qquad \underline{Answer:} \quad \boxed{B}$$

Solution #10

Find: LL ← liquid limit

Given: $M_{Dish}=0.13\,[lb]$ ← mass of the dish

Liquid Limit Test Data

Sample	$M_{Moist\ Soil\ \&\ Dish}$	$M_{Dry\ Soil\ \&\ Dish}$	# Turns
1	2.41 [lb]	1.68 [lb]	12
2	2.45 [lb]	1.82 [lb]	22
3	2.39 [lb]	1.88 [lb]	37

A) 28
B) 34
C) 41
D) 48

Analysis:

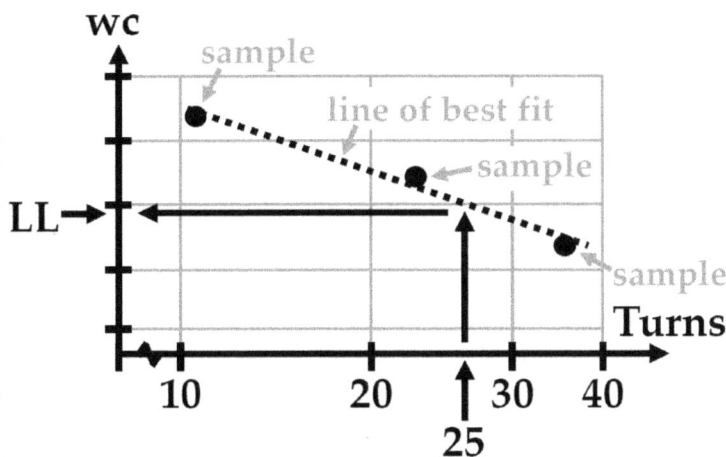

Figure 1

Figure 1 shows how to graphically identify the liquid limit of a soil.
i) Plot the water content vs. the number of turns on a semi-log plot.
ii) Sketch a line of best fit.
iii) Sketch vertically upward from the horizontal axis where Turns=25 to the line of best fit, then from that point sketch left to the vertical axis.
iv) The Liquid Limit is the water content associated 25 turns on the line of best fit.

Eq. 2, 3 and 4 calculates the water content of samples 1, 2 and 3.

$$wc_1=\frac{M_{1,W}}{M_{1,S}} \leftarrow eq.2 \qquad wc_2=\frac{M_{2,W}}{M_{2,S}} \leftarrow eq.3 \qquad wc_3=\frac{M_{3,W}}{M_{3,S}} \leftarrow eq.4$$

Eq. 5, 6 and 7 calculate the mass of the water in the sample by subtracting the mass of the dry sample from the mass of the moist sample.

$$M_{1,W}=M_{1,Moist\ Soil\ \&\ Dish}-M_{1,Dry\ Soil\ \&\ Dish} \leftarrow eq.5$$

$M_{1,Moist\ Soil\ \&\ Dish}=2.41\,[lb]$
$M_{1,Dry\ Soil\ \&\ Dish}=1.68\,[lb]$

Solution #10 (cont.)

$M_{1,W} = 2.41\,[\text{lb}] - 1.68\,[\text{lb}]$

$M_{1,W} = 0.73\,[\text{lb}]$

Plug in the appropriate masses into eq. 4, 5 and 6, then compute the mass of water in each sample.

$M_{2,W} = M_{2,\text{Moist Soil \& Dish}} - M_{2,\text{Dry Soil \& Dish}} \leftarrow eq.\,5$

$\quad M_{2,\text{Moist Soil \& Dish}} = 2.45\,[\text{lb}]$
$\quad\quad M_{2,\text{Dry Soil \& Dish}} = 1.82\,[\text{lb}]$

$M_{2,W} = 2.45\,[\text{lb}] - 1.82\,[\text{lb}]$

$M_{2,W} = 0.63\,[\text{lb}]$

$M_{3,W} = M_{3,\text{Moist Soil \& Dish}} - M_{3,\text{Dry Soil \& Dish}} \leftarrow eq.\,6$

$\quad M_{2,\text{Moist Soil \& Dish}} = 2.39\,[\text{lb}]$
$\quad\quad M_{3,\text{Dry Soil \& Dish}} = 1.88\,[\text{lb}]$

$M_{3,W} = 2.39\,[\text{lb}] - 1.88\,[\text{lb}]$

$M_{3,W} = 0.51\,[\text{lb}]$

$M_{1,S} = M_{1,\text{Dry Soil \& Dish}} - M_{\text{Dish}} \leftarrow eq.\,7$

$\quad M_{1,\text{Dry Soil \& Dish}} = 1.68\,[\text{lb}] \quad M_{\text{Dish}} = 0.13\,[\text{lb}]$

Plug in the appropriate masses into eq. 7, 8 and 9, then compute the mass of solid material in each sample.

$M_{1,S} = 1.68\,[\text{lb}] - 0.13\,[\text{lb}]$

$M_{1,S} = 1.55\,[\text{lb}]$

$M_{2,S} = M_{2,\text{Dry Soil \& Dish}} - M_{\text{Dish}} \leftarrow eq.\,8$

$\quad M_{2,\text{Dry Soil \& Dish}} = 1.82\,[\text{lb}] \quad M_{\text{Dish}} = 0.13\,[\text{lb}]$

$M_{2,S} = 1.82\,[\text{lb}] - 0.13\,[\text{lb}]$

$M_{2,S} = 1.69\,[\text{lb}]$

$M_{3,S} = M_{1,\text{Dry Soil \& Dish}} - M_{\text{Dish}} \leftarrow eq.\,9$

$\quad M_{3,\text{Dry Soil \& Dish}} = 1.88\,[\text{lb}] \quad M_{\text{Dish}} = 0.13\,[\text{lb}]$

Solution #10 (cont.)

$M_{3,S} = 1.88 \, [lb] - 0.13 \, [lb]$

$M_{3,S} = 1.75 \, [lb]$

Plug in the known values into eq. 1, 2 and 3, then solve for wc_1, wc_2 and wc_3.

$M_{1,W} = 0.73 \, [lb]$ $M_{2,W} = 0.63 \, [lb]$ $M_{3,W} = 0.51 \, [lb]$

$$wc_1 = \frac{M_{1,W}}{M_{1,S}} \leftarrow eq.1 \qquad wc_2 = \frac{M_{2,W}}{M_{2,S}} \leftarrow eq.2 \qquad wc_3 = \frac{M_{3,W}}{M_{3,S}} \leftarrow eq.3$$

$M_{1,S} = 1.55 \, [lb]$ $M_{2,S} = 1.69 \, [lb]$ $M_{3,S} = 1.75 \, [lb]$

$$wc_1 = \frac{0.73 \, [lb]}{1.55 \, [lb]} \qquad wc_2 = \frac{0.63 \, [lb]}{1.69 \, [lb]} \qquad wc_3 = \frac{0.51 \, [lb]}{1.75 \, [lb]}$$

$$wc_1 = 0.471 \qquad wc_2 = 0.373 \qquad wc_3 = 0.291$$

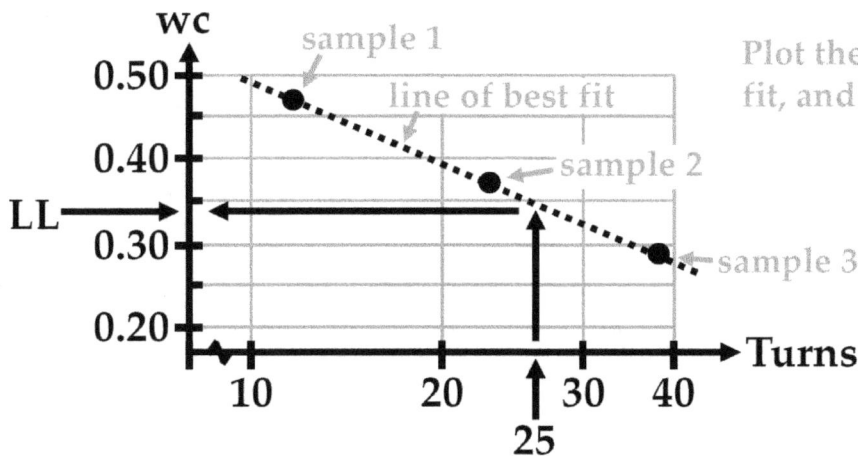

Plot the data, sketch the line of best fit, and determine the liquid limit.

Figure 2

$LL = 0.34$

Answer: B

Civil Engineering Practice Examination #2

Solution #11

Find: h_b ← beam height

Given:

$L = 9 \, [\text{ft}]$ ← beam length

$w_b = 6 \, [\text{in}]$ ← beam width

$E = 2.9 * 10^7 \, [\text{lb/in}^2]$ ← elastic modulus

$y_{max} = 0.059 \, [\text{in}]$

maximum deflection in the beam caused by the loading

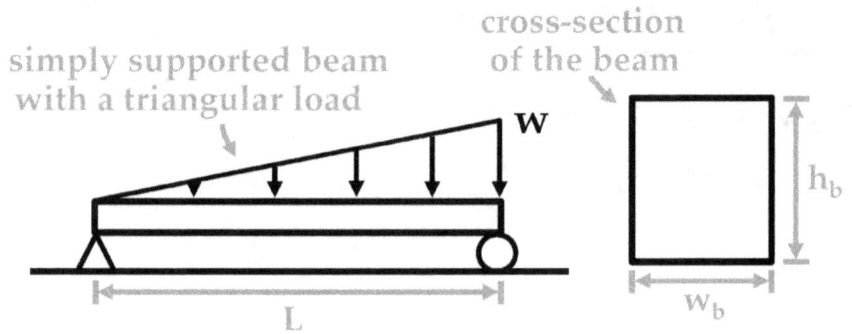

simply supported beam with a triangular load

cross-section of the beam

w

L

w_b

h_b

$w = 20 \, [\text{k/ft}]$

loading at the far right end of the beam

A) 6 [in]

B) 8 [in]

C) 9 [in]

D) 12 [in]

Analysis:

beam width   beam height

$$I = \frac{w_b * h_b{}^3}{12} \leftarrow eq.1$$

Eq. 1 computes the area moment of inertia of the beam, which has a rectangular cross-section.

$$h_b = \left(\frac{12 * I}{w_b} \right)^{1/3} \leftarrow eq.2$$

Solve eq. 1 for the beam height, h_b

maximum loading   beam length

$$y_{max} = 0.00652 * \left(\frac{w * L^4}{E * I} \right) \leftarrow eq.3$$

elastic modulus   area moment of inertia

Eq. 3 computes the maximum deflection in a simply supported beam subjected to a triangular load.

$$I = 0.00652 * \left(\frac{w * L^4}{E * y_{max}} \right) \leftarrow eq.4$$

Solve eq. 3 for the area moment of inertia, I.

$$w = 20 \, [\text{k/ft}] * 1{,}000 \left[\frac{\text{lb}}{\text{k}} \right] \leftarrow eq.5$$

Eq. 5 converts the load to units of pounds per foot.

$$w = 20{,}000 \, [\text{lb/ft}]$$

46

Solution #11 (cont.)

$w = 20,000\,[\text{lb/ft}]$ $L = 9\,[\text{ft}]$

$$I = 0.00652 * \left(\frac{w * L^4}{E * y_{max}}\right) \leftarrow eq.\,4$$

$E = 2.9 * 10^7\,[\text{lb/in}^2]$ $y_{max} = 0.059\,[\text{in}]$

Plug in variables w, L, E and y_{max} into eq. 4, then solve for I.

$$I = 0.00652 * \left(\frac{20,000\,[\text{lb/ft}] * (9\,[\text{ft}])^4}{2.9 * 10^7\,[\text{lb/in}^2] * 0.059\,[\text{in}]}\right)$$

$$I = 0.500\,[\text{ft}^3 * \text{in}] * \left(12\left[\frac{\text{in}}{\text{ft}}\right]\right)^3 \leftarrow eq.\,6$$

Eq. 6 converts the area moment of inertia to units of inches to the fourth power.

$$I = 864\,[\text{in}^4]$$

$I = 864\,[\text{in}^4]$

$$h_b = \left(\frac{12 * I}{w_b}\right)^{1/3} \leftarrow eq.\,2$$

$w_b = 6\,[\text{in}]$

Plug in variables I and w_b into eq. 2, then solve for h_b.

$$h_b = \left(\frac{12 * 864\,[\text{in}^4]}{6\,[\text{in}]}\right)^{1/3}$$

$$h_b = 12\,[\text{in}]$$

Answer: $\boxed{\text{D}}$

Civil Engineering Practice Examination #2

Solution #12

Find: F_R ←—the reaction force required to hold the vane stationary

Given:

$Q = 0.25 \, [\text{m}^3/\text{s}]$
flow rate

$v = 15 \, [\text{m/s}]$ ←—velocity of flow

$\varrho = 750 \, [\text{kg/m}^3]$ ←—density of the fluid

$\theta = 38°$ ←—deflection angle

neglect all forces caused by gravity and (static) pressure

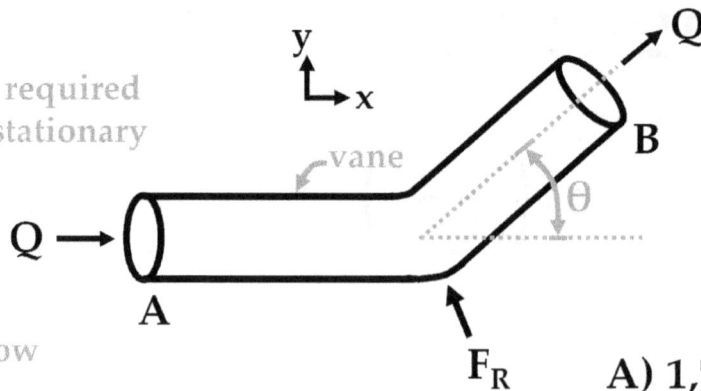

A) 1,730 [N]
B) 1,830 [N]
C) 5,030 [N]
D) 5,320 [N]

Analysis:

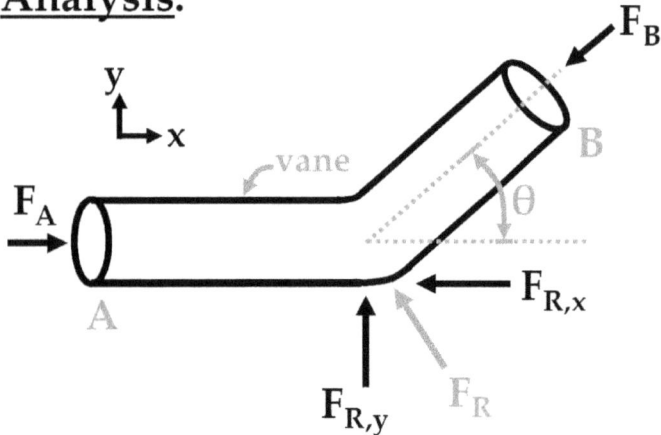

Figure 1

The reaction force is broken down into horizontal and vertical components.

Figure 1 shows a free body diagram of the vane and identifies the hydraulic forces (F_A, F_B) and reaction forces ($F_{R,y}$, $F_{R,x}$).

$$F_R = \sqrt{F_{R,x}^2 + F_{R,y}^2} \quad \text{←}eq.1$$

horizontal reaction force   vertical reaction force

Eq. 1 computes the reaction force F_R.

$$\Sigma F_x = 0 = F_A - F_{R,x} - F_B * \cos(\theta) \quad \text{←}eq.2$$

hydraulic force of the water acting on the vane at ends A and B

Eq. 2 sets the sum of the horizontal forces equal to zero.

$$F_{R,x} = F_A - F_B * \cos(\theta) \quad \text{←}eq.3$$

Solve eq. 2 for $F_{R,x}$.

Solution #12 (cont.)

$$\varrho=750\,[kg/m^3] \qquad v=15\,[m/s]$$

$$F_A=F_B=\varrho*Q*v \; \leftarrow eq.4$$

$$Q=0.25\,[m^3/s]$$

Eq.4 computes the hydraulic forces F_A and F_B.

Plug in variables ϱ, Q and v into eq.4, then solve for forces F_A and F_B.

$$F_A=F_B=750\,[kg/m^3]*0.25\,[m^3/s]*15\,[m/s]$$

$$F_A=F_B=2{,}813\left[\frac{kg*m}{s^2}\right]*1\left[\frac{N*s^2}{kg*m}\right]$$

Convert the force to Newtons.

conversion factor

$$F_A=F_B=2{,}813\,[N]$$

$$F_{R,x}=F_A-F_B*\cos(\theta) \; \leftarrow eq.3$$

$$F_A=F_B=2{,}813\,[N] \qquad \theta=38°$$

Plug in variables F_A, F_B and θ into eq.3, then solve for $F_{R,x}$.

$$F_{R,x}=2{,}813\,[N]-2{,}813\,[N]*\cos(38°)$$

$$F_{R,x}=596\,[N]$$

$$\Sigma F_y=0=F_{R,y}-F_B*\sin(\theta) \; \leftarrow eq.5$$

Eq.5 sets the sum of the vertical forces equal to zero.

$$F_{R,y}=F_B*\sin(\theta) \; \leftarrow eq.6$$

$$F_B=2{,}813\,[N] \qquad \theta=38°$$

Solve eq.5 for $F_{R,y}$. Plug in variables F_B and θ into eq.6, then solve for $F_{R,y}$.

$$F_{R,y}=2{,}813\,[N]*\sin(38°)$$

$$F_{R,y}=1{,}732\,[N]$$

Solution #12 (cont.)

$$F_R = \sqrt{F_{R,x}^2 + F_{R,y}^2} \leftarrow eq.\,1$$

$F_{R,x} = 596\,[N]$ $F_{R,y} = 1{,}732\,[N]$

Plug in variables $F_{R,x}$ and $F_{R,y}$ into eq. 1, then solve for F_R.

$$F_R = \sqrt{(596\,[N])^2 + (1{,}732\,[N])^2}$$

$$F_R = 1{,}832\,[N]$$

Answer: $\boxed{B}$

Solution #13

<u>Find:</u> $s_{2,s}$ ← stopping distance of vehicle 2

<u>Given:</u> $G=0$ ← grade

$v_{1,i}=25\,[\text{mi/hr}]$ ← initial velocity of vehicle 1

$t_{1,r}=1.5\,[\text{s}]$ ← reaction time of vehicle 1 $v_{2,i}=55\,[\text{mi/hr}]$

$s_{1,b}=114.6\,[\text{ft}]$ ← stopping distance of vehicle 1

initial velocity of vehicle 2

A) 250 [ft]

$t_{2,r}=2.0\,[\text{s}]$ B) 390 [ft]

reaction time   C) 560 [ft]
of vehicle 2   D) 720 [ft]

Analysis:

stopping distance → $s_s=s_r+s_b$ ← eq.1   Eq.1 calculates the stopping distance.

reaction distance   breaking distance

$s_{2,s}=s_{2,r}+s_{2,b}$ ← eq.2   Add the subscript "2" to each term of eq.1 to specify vehicle 2.

$s_{2,r}=v_{2,i}*t_{2,r}$ ← eq.3   Eq.3 computes the reaction distance traveled by vehicle 2.

initial velocity   reaction time

$$v_{2,i}=55\left[\frac{\text{mi}}{\text{hr}}\right]*5{,}280\left[\frac{\text{ft}}{\text{mi}}\right]*\frac{1}{3{,}600}\left[\frac{\text{hr}}{\text{s}}\right] \leftarrow eq.4$$

Eq. 4 converts the initial velocity to feet per second.

$$v_{2,i}=80.67\left[\frac{\text{ft}}{\text{s}}\right]$$

$v_{2,i}=80.67\,[\text{ft/s}]$ $t_{2,r}=2.0\,[\text{s}]$

$s_{2,r}=v_{2,i}*t_{2,r}$ ← eq.3

Plug in variables $v_{2,i}$ and $t_{2,r}$ into eq.3, then solve for $s_{2,r}$.

$s_{2,r}=80.67\,[\text{ft/s}]*2.0\,[\text{s}]$

Solution #13 (cont.)

$$s_{2,r} = 161.34 \, [\text{ft}]$$

$$s_{2,b} = \frac{v_{2,i}^2 - v_{2,f}^2}{2 * g * (f + G)} \leftarrow eq.5$$

gravitational acceleration — friction factor — grade

Eq. 5 computes the breaking distance of vehicle 2.

Use data from vehicle 1 to determine the friction factor.

$$s_{1,b} = \frac{v_{1,i}^2 - v_{1,f}^2}{2 * g * (f + G)} \leftarrow eq.6$$

Eq. 6 computes the breaking distance of vehicle 1.

Solve eq. 6 for the friction factor, f.

$$f = \frac{v_{1,i}^2 - v_{1,f}^2}{2 * g * s_{1,b}} - G \leftarrow eq.7$$

$$v_{1,i} = 25 \left[\frac{\text{mi}}{\text{hr}}\right] * 5{,}280 \left[\frac{\text{ft}}{\text{mi}}\right] * \frac{1}{3{,}600} \left[\frac{\text{hr}}{\text{s}}\right] \leftarrow eq.8$$

Eq. 8 converts the initial velocity of vehicle 1 to feet per second.

$$v_{1,i} = 36.67 \left[\frac{\text{ft}}{\text{s}}\right]$$

$v_{1,i} = 36.67 \, [\text{ft/s}]$ $v_{1,f} = 0 \, [\text{ft/s}]$

$$f = \frac{v_{1,i}^2 - v_{1,f}^2}{2 * g * s_{1,b}} - G \leftarrow eq.7$$

$g = 32.2 \, [\text{ft/s}^2]$ $G = 0 \, [\text{ft}]$ $s_{1,b} = 114.6 \, [\text{ft}]$

Plug in variables $v_{1,i}$, $v_{1,f}$, g, $s_{1,b}$ and G into eq.7, then solve for f.

$$f = \frac{(36.67 \, [\text{ft/s}])^2 - (0 \, [\text{ft/s}])^2}{2 * 32.2 [\text{ft/s}^2] * 114.6 \, [\text{ft}]} - 0$$

$$f = 0.182$$

Solution #13 (cont.)

$v_{2,i}=80.67\,[\text{ft/s}]$ $v_{2,f}=0\,[\text{ft/s}]$

$$s_{2,b}=\frac{v_{2,i}^{2}-v_{2,f}^{2}}{2*g*(f+G)} \leftarrow eq.5$$

$G=0\,[\text{ft}]$

$g=32.2\,[\text{ft/s}^2]$ $f=0.182$

Plug in variables $v_{2,i}$, $v_{2,i}$, g, $s_{2,b}$ and G into eq.5, then solve for f.

$$s_{2,b}=\frac{(80.67\,[\text{ft/s}])^{2}-(0\,[\text{ft/s}])^{2}}{2*32.2\,[\text{ft/s}^2]*(0.182+0)}$$

$$s_{2,b}=555.2\,[\text{ft}]$$

$s_{2,r}=161.34\,[\text{ft}]$ $s_{2,b}=555.2\,[\text{ft}]$

$$s_{2,s}=s_{2,r}+s_{2,b} \leftarrow eq.2$$

Plug in variables $s_{2,r}$ and $s_{2,b}$ into eq.2, then solve for $s_{2,s}$.

$$s_{2,s}=161.34\,[\text{ft}]+555.2\,[\text{ft}]$$

$$s_{2,s}=716.5\,[\text{ft}]$$

Answer: $\boxed{\text{D}}$

Civil Engineering Practice Examination #2

Solution #14

Find: The Critical Path

Given:

$$ES_A = 1$$

the early start
of Activity A

$$ES_B = 1$$

the early start
of Activity B

ID	Duration	Pred
A	1	-
B	4	-
C	5	A
D	1	A,B
E	8	B,D
F	6	C
G	4	D,E,F

predecessor
activities

A) A-C-F-G

B) A-D-E-G

C) B-D-E-G

D) B-D-G

Analysis:

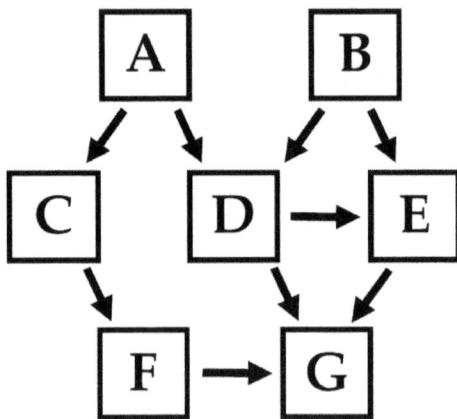

Figure 1

Figure 1 identifies the predecessor/
successor relationships between the
different activities within the schedule.

Activities A and B have no predecessor
activities, and Activity G has no successor
activities.

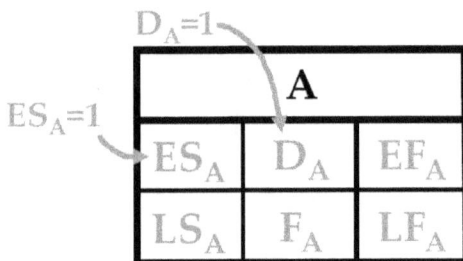

Figure 2

Figure 2 shows the box diagram
template, for Activity A. Where each
box represents a time, or time period:

ES = early start
D = duration
EF = early finish
LS = late start
F = float
LF = late finish

$$EF_A = ES_A + D_A \leftarrow eq.1$$

Plug in ES_A and D_A, into
eq.1, then solve for EF_A.

Solution #14 (cont.)

$$EF_A = 1 + 1$$

$$EF_A = 2$$

$$\overset{ES_B=1}{}\qquad\overset{D_B=4}{}$$

$$EF_B = ES_B + D_B \leftarrow eq.\,2$$

$$EF_B = 1 + 4$$

$$EF_B = 5$$

The early finish of an activity equals the early start of an activity plus the duration of that activity.

The problem statement provides the duration of all 7 activities.

Plug in ES_B and D_B, into eq.2, then solve for EF_B.

The early start of an activity equals the latest early finish of all it's predecessor activities.

Eq. 3 and eq. 4 compute the early start of activity C and activity D, respectively.

Eq. 5 and eq. 6 compute the early finish of activity C and activity D, respectively.

$$\overset{EF_A=2}{}\qquad\qquad\overset{EF_B=5}{}$$

A		
1	1	2
LS_A	F_A	LF_A

B		
1	4	5
LS_B	F_B	LF_B

Figure 3

$$\overset{EF_A=2}{}$$

$$ES_C = \max(EF_A) \leftarrow eq.\,3$$

$$ES_C = \max(2)$$

$$ES_C = 2$$

$$\overset{EF_A=2}{}\qquad\overset{EF_B=5}{}$$

$$ES_D = \max(EF_A, EF_B) \leftarrow eq.\,4$$

$$ES_D = \max(2,5)$$

$$ES_D = 5$$

$$\overset{ES_C=2}{}\qquad\overset{D_C=5}{}$$

$$EF_C = ES_C + D_C \leftarrow eq.\,5$$

$$EF_C = 2 + 5$$

$$EF_C = 7$$

$$\overset{ES_D=5}{}\qquad\overset{D_D=1}{}$$

$$EF_D = ES_D + D_D \leftarrow eq.\,6$$

$$EF_D = 5 + 1$$

$$EF_D = 6$$

Civil Engineering Practice Examination #2

Solution #14 (cont.)

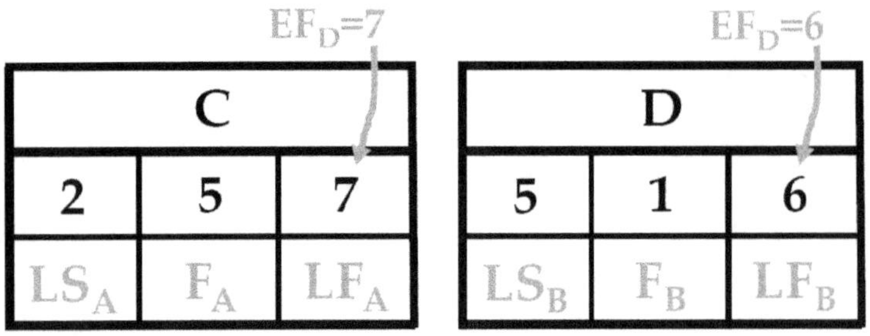

	C	
2	5	7
LS_A	F_A	LF_A

$EF_D=7$

	D	
5	1	6
LS_B	F_B	LF_B

$EF_D=6$

Figure 4

Plug in the early finish for activities C and D.

Eq.7 and eq.8 compute the early start of activity F and activity E, respectively.

Eq.9 and eq.10 compute the early finish of activity F and activity E, respectively.

$EF_C=7$

$$ES_F=\max(EF_C) \leftarrow eq.7$$
$$ES_F=\max(7)$$
$$ES_F=7$$

$EF_B=5 \quad EF_D=6$

$$ES_E=\max(EF_B,EF_D) \leftarrow eq.8$$
$$ES_E=\max(5,6)$$
$$ES_E=6$$

$ES_F=7 \quad D_F=6$

$$EF_F=ES_F+D_F \leftarrow eq.9$$
$$EF_F=7+6$$
$$EF_F=13$$

$ES_E=6 \quad D_E=8$

$$EF_E=ES_E+D_E \leftarrow eq.10$$
$$EF_E=6+8$$
$$EF_E=14$$

$EF_D=6 \quad EF_E=14 \quad EF_F=13$

$$ES_G=\max(EF_D,EF_E,EF_F) \leftarrow eq.11$$
$$ES_G=\max(6,14,13)$$
$$ES_G=14$$

Eq.11 computes the early start of activity G. Plug in variables EF_D, EF_E and EF_F, then solve for ES_G.

The maximum value between 6, 14 and 13, is 14.

Now that we know ES_G, we can trace back through the schedule to determine the critical path.

Solution #14 (cont.)

The critical path occurs through the activities which have 0 float.

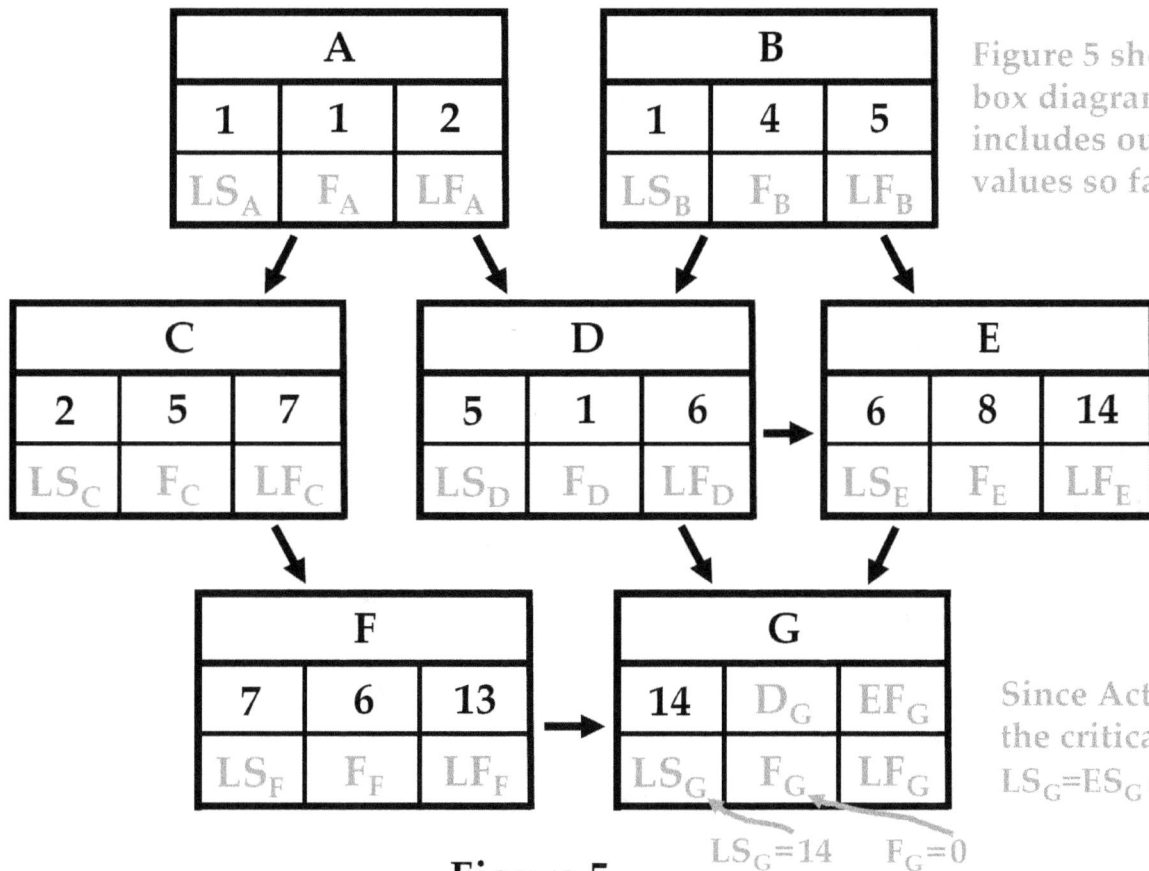

Figure 5 shows the full box diagram, and includes our calculated values so far.

A		
1	1	2
LS_A	F_A	LF_A

B		
1	4	5
LS_B	F_B	LF_B

C		
2	5	7
LS_C	F_C	LF_C

D		
5	1	6
LS_D	F_D	LF_D

E		
6	8	14
LS_E	F_E	LF_E

F		
7	6	13
LS_F	F_F	LF_F

G		
14	D_G	EF_G
LS_G	F_G	LF_G

$LS_G=14$ $F_G=0$

Figure 5

Since Activity G is on the critical path, $LS_G=ES_G$ and $F_G=0$.

Tracing back, the latest finish of an activity equals the earliest late start of all of it's successor activities.

$$LS_G=14$$
$$LF_E=LF_F=\min(LS_G) \leftarrow eq.12$$

$$LF_E=LF_F=\min(14)$$

$$LF_E=LF_F=14$$

Eq.12 calculates the late finish of activities E and F. Plug in variable LS_G into eq.12, then solve for LF_E and LF_F.

Eq.13 and eq.14 compute the float of activities E and F by subtracting the early finish from the late finish.

$$LF_E=14 \quad EF_E=14$$
$$F_E=LF_E-EF_E \leftarrow eq.13$$

$$F_E=14-14$$

$$F_E=0$$

$$LF_F=14 \quad EF_F=13$$
$$F_F=LF_F-EF_F \leftarrow eq.14$$

$$F_F=14-13$$

$$F_F=1$$

Plug in variables LF_E, EF_E, LF_F and EF_F into eq.13 and eq.14, and solve for F_E and F_E.

Civil Engineering Practice Examination #2

Solution #14 (cont.)

Since the float of activity E equals zero, we know activity E is on the critical path.

$$LS_E = LF_E - D_E \leftarrow eq.15$$

$$LS_E = 14 - 8$$

$$LS_E = 6$$

Eq. 15 computes the late start of activity E. Plug in variables L_{FE} and D_E into eq.15, then solve for LS_E.

Plug in variables LS_E and LS_G into eq.16, then solve for LF_D.

$$LF_D = \min(LS_E, LS_G) \leftarrow eq.16$$

$$LF_D = \min(6,14)$$

$$LF_D = 6$$

Plug in variables LF_D and EF_D into eq.17, then solve for F_D.

$$F_D = LF_D - EF_D \leftarrow eq.17$$

$$F_D = 6 - 6$$

$$F_D = 0$$

Plug in variables LF_D and D_D into eq.18, then solve for LS_D.

$$LS_D = LF_D - D_D \leftarrow eq.18$$

$$LS_D = 6 - 1$$

$$LS_D = 5$$

Plug in variables LS_D and LS_E into eq.19, then solve for LF_B.

$$LF_B = \min(LS_D, LS_E) \leftarrow eq.19$$

$$LF_B = \min(5,6)$$

$$LF_B = 5$$

Plug in variables LF_B and EF_B into eq.20, then solve for F_B.

$$F_B = LF_B - EF_B \leftarrow eq.20$$

$$F_B = 5 - 5$$

$$F_B = 0$$

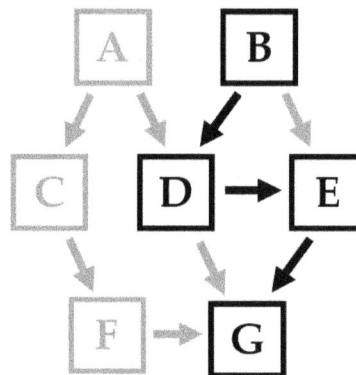

Figure 6 highlights the critical path of the schedule.

Answer: C

Figure 6

Solution #15

<u>Find:</u> F_{GC} ← the force in member GC

<u>Given:</u>

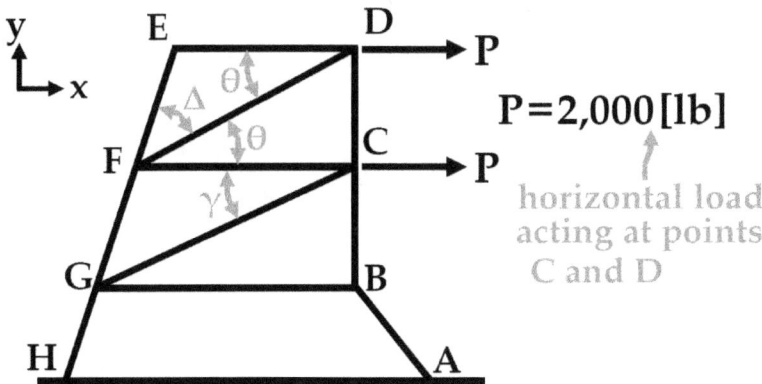

$\left.\begin{array}{l}\theta=37.6° \\ \Delta=49.3° \\ \gamma=32.0°\end{array}\right\}$ interior angles of the structure

$P=2{,}000\,[lb]$

horizontal load acting at points C and D

A) 4,180 [lb] (tension)

B) 4,620 [lb] (tension)

C) 4,180 [lb] (compression)

D) 4,620 [lb] (compression)

<u>Analysis:</u>

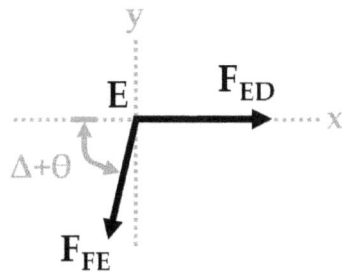

Figure 1

Figure 1 shows the forces acting at joint E.

Positive forces pointing away from the joint are assumed to be in tension.

$$\Sigma F_y=0=-F_{FE}*\sin(\Delta+\theta) \leftarrow eq.1$$

$$F_{FE}=0\,[lb]$$

Eq.1 sums the forces at joint E in the vertical direction.

Solve eq.1 for force F_{FE}.

$$\Sigma F_x=0=-F_{FE}*\cos(\Delta+\theta)+F_{ED} \leftarrow eq.2$$

Eq.2 sums the forces at joint E in the horizontal direction.

$$F_{ED}=F_{FE}*\cos(\Delta+\theta)$$

$\theta=37.6°$

$F_{FE}=0\,[lb]$ $\Delta=49.3°$

Solve eq.2 for force F_{ED}, plug in variables F_{FE}, θ and Δ, then solve for F_{ED}.

$$F_{ED}=0\,[lb]*\cos(49.3°+37.6°)$$

$$F_{ED}=0\,[lb]$$

Civil Engineering Practice Examination #2

Solution #15 (cont.)

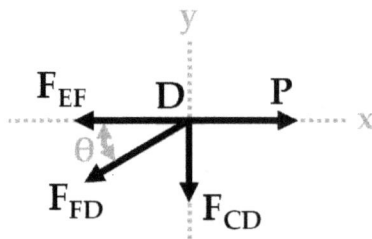

Figure 2

Figure 2 shows the forces acting at joint D.

Eq.3 sums the forces at joint D in the horizontal direction.

$$\Sigma F_x = 0 = P - F_{FE} - F_{FD} * \cos(\theta) \leftarrow eq.3$$

Solve eq.3 for force F_{FD}.

$$P = 2,000\,[lb] \qquad F_{FE} = 0\,[lb]$$

$$F_{FD} = \frac{P - F_{FE}}{\cos(\theta)} \leftarrow eq.4$$

$$\theta = 37.6°$$

Plug in variables P, F_{FE} and θ into eq.4, then solve for force F_{FD}.

$$F_{FD} = \frac{2,000\,[lb] - 0\,[lb]}{\cos(37.6°)}$$

$$F_{FD} = 2,524\,[lb]$$

Since force F_{FD} is pointing away from the joint, member FD is in tension.

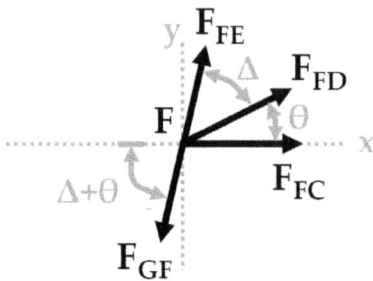

Figure 3

Figure 3 shows the forces acting at joint F.

Eq.5 sums the forces at joint F in the vertical direction.

$$\Sigma F_y = 0 = -F_{GF} * \sin(\Delta + \theta) + F_{FE} * \sin(\Delta + \theta) + F_{FD} * \sin(\theta) \leftarrow eq.5$$

$$F_{FE} = 0\,[lb] \qquad\qquad \theta = 37.6°$$

$$F_{GF} = \frac{F_{FE} * \sin(\Delta + \theta) + F_{FD} * \sin(\theta)}{\sin(\Delta + \theta)}$$

$$\Delta = 49.3° \qquad\qquad F_{FD} = 2,524\,[lb]$$

Solve eq.5 for F_{GF}, then plug in variables F_{FE}, Δ, θ and F_{FD}, then solve for F_{GF}.

Solution #15 (cont.)

$$F_{GF} = \frac{0\,[lb]*\sin(49.3°+37.6°)+2{,}524\,[lb]*\sin(37.6°)}{\sin(49.3°+37.6°)}$$

$$F_{GF}=1{,}542\,[lb]$$

Eq. 6 sums the forces at joint F in the horizontal direction.

$$\Sigma F_x=0=F_{FC}+F_{FD}*\cos(\theta)+F_{FE}*\cos(\Delta+\theta)-F_{GF}*\cos(\Delta+\theta) \quad \leftarrow eq.\,6$$

Solve eq. 6 for force F_{FC}.

$$\underset{F_{GF}=1{,}542\,[lb]}{F_{FC}}=F_{GF}*\underset{\Delta=49.3°}{\cos(\Delta+\theta)}-F_{FD}*\underset{\theta=37.6°}{\cos(\theta)}-\underset{F_{FE}=0\,[lb]}{F_{FE}}*\underset{\Delta=49.3°\ \ \theta=37.6°}{\cos(\Delta+\theta)} \quad \leftarrow eq.\,7$$

$$F_{FC}=1{,}542\,[lb]*\cos(49.3°+37.6°)-2{,}524\,[lb]*\cos(37.6°)$$
$$-0\,[lb]*\cos(49.3°+37.6°)$$

Plug in variables F_{GF}, Δ, θ and F_{FE} into eq. 7, then solve for F_{FC}.

$$F_{FC}=-1{,}916\,[lb]$$

Since the assumed tensile force in member FC computes to a negative value, we know member FC is actually in compression.

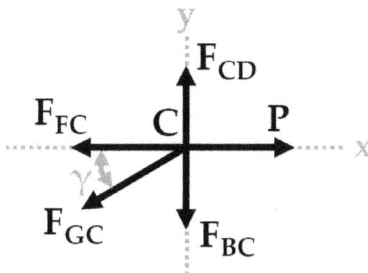

Figure 4

Figure 4 shows the forces acting at joint C.

Eq. 8 sums the forces at joint C in the horizontal direction.

$$\Sigma F_x=0=P-F_{FC}-F_{GC}*\cos(\gamma) \quad \leftarrow eq.\,8$$

$$\underset{P=2{,}000\,[lb]}{} \qquad \underset{F_{FC}=-1{,}916\,[lb]}{}$$

$$F_{GC}=\frac{P-F_{FC}}{\cos(\gamma)} \quad \leftarrow eq.\,9$$

$$\gamma=32.0°$$

Solve eq. 9 for F_{GC}, then plug in variables P, γ and F_{FC} into eq. 8 and solve for F_{GC}.

Solution #15 (cont.)

$$F_{GC} = \frac{2{,}000\,[\text{lb}] - (-1{,}916\,[\text{lb}])}{\cos(32.0^\circ)}$$

$$F_{GC} = 4{,}618\,[\text{lb}]$$
(tension)

Since the force in member GC is positive and pointing away from the joint, then the force in member GC is in tension.

Answer: $\boxed{\text{B}}$

Solution #16

<u>Find</u>: Q_p ← peak runoff flow rate

<u>Given</u>: 20-year storm event

total runoff area →

park →

residential

$i\,[in/hr]$ $d=60\,[min]$ ← storm duration

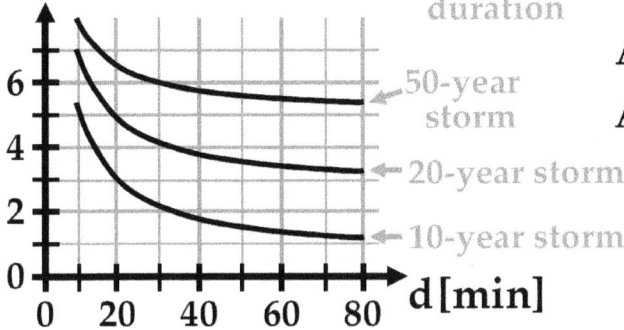

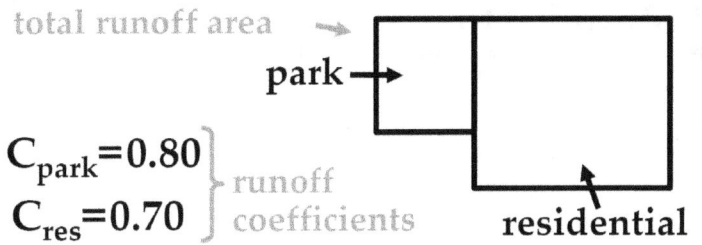

$C_{park}=0.80$ ⎤ runoff
$C_{res}=0.70$ ⎦ coefficients

$A_{park}=5\,[acres]$ ⎤ watershed areas
$A_{res}=15\,[acres]$ ⎦

$t_c=40\,[min]$
time of concentration

(graph: $i\,[in/hr]$ vs $d\,[min]$, curves labeled 50-year storm, 20-year storm, 10-year storm; y-axis 0,2,4,6; x-axis 0,20,40,60,80)

A) $17\,[ft^3/s]$

B) $38\,[ft^3/s]$

C) $51\,[ft^3/s]$

D) $85\,[ft^3/s]$

Analysis:

peak runoff flow rate [cfs]

rainfall intensity [in/hr]

watershed area [acres]

$$Q_p=K*C*i*A \leftarrow eq.1$$

unit conversion coefficient

composite runoff coefficient

Eq. 1 computes the peak runoff flowrate.

$$K=1.0083\left[\frac{ft^3*hr}{s*in*acre}\right] \leftarrow eq.2$$

Eq. 2 shows the unit conversion coefficient for English units.

runoff coefficient of part i

$$C=\frac{\Sigma C_i*A_i}{\Sigma A_i} \leftarrow eq.3$$

composite runoff coefficient

area of part i

Eq. 3 computes the composite runoff coefficient of the entire watershed.

$C_{park}=0.80$ $C_{res}=0.70$

$$C=\frac{C_{park}*A_{park}+C_{res}*A_{res}}{A_{park}+A_{res}} \leftarrow eq.4$$

$A_{park}=5\,[acres]$ $A_{res}=15\,[acres]$

Expand the summation terms in eq. 3 to account for the park area and the residential area.

Plug in C_{park}, A_{park}, C_{res} and A_{res} into eq. 4, then solve for C.

$$C=\frac{0.80*5\,[acres]+0.70*15\,[acres]}{5\,[acres]+15\,[acres]}$$

Solution #16 (cont.)

$$C=0.725$$

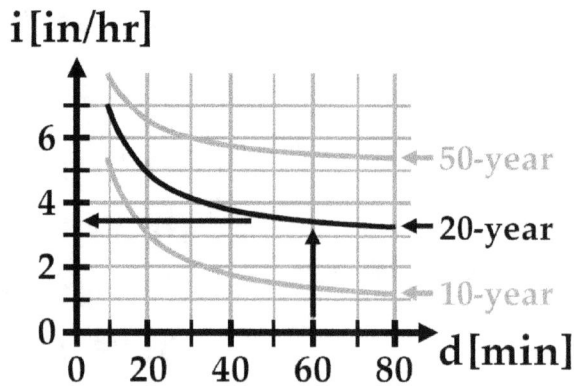

Figure 1

Figure 1 shows the intensity-duration-frequency graph for the 10-year, 20-year and 50-year return periods.

For a storm duration of 60 minutes, trace up to the 20-year return period line, then trace left to the intensity axis to find i.

$$\left.\begin{array}{c} \text{20-year storm} \\ d=60\,[\text{min}] \end{array}\right\} \rightarrow \underline{\text{IDF curve}}$$

$$\downarrow$$

$$i=3.5\,[\text{in/hr}]$$

Based on the IDF curve, the storm intensity is 3.5 inches per hour.

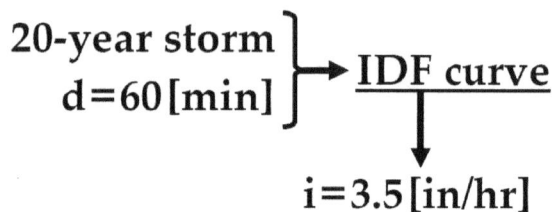

$$A=A_{park}+A_{res} \leftarrow eq.5$$

$$A=5\,[\text{acres}]+15\,[\text{acres}]$$

$$A=20\,[\text{acres}]$$

Eq.5 computes the total area of the watershed.

$$K=1.0083\left[\frac{ft^3 * hr}{s*in*acre}\right] \quad A=20\,[\text{acres}]$$

$$Q_p=K*C*i*A \leftarrow eq.1$$

$$C=0.725 \qquad i=3.5\,[\text{in/hr}]$$

Plug in variables K, C, i and A into eq.1, then solve for Q_p.

$$Q_p=1.0083\left[\frac{ft^3 * hr}{s*in*acre}\right]*0.725*3.5\left[\frac{in}{hr}\right]*20\,[\text{acres}]$$

$$Q_p=51.2\,[ft^3/s] \qquad \underline{\text{Answer:}} \quad \boxed{C}$$

Solution #17

assume there is no swell
or shrinkage of the soil

Find: C ← total cost of transporting soil

Given: R=$0.01[ft⁻⁴] ← unit cost of transporting soil
per cubic foot volume, per
foot of distance traveled

$w=15[ft]$
↑
constant width of
the soil pile and
fill pit (into and
out of the page)

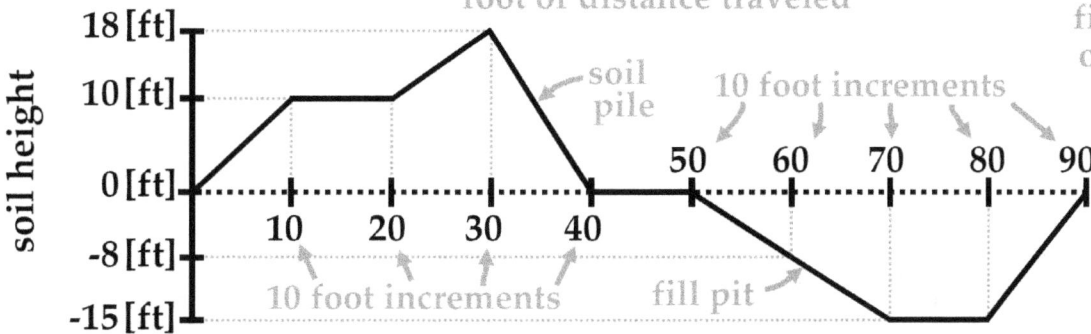

soil pile

10 foot increments

10 foot increments

fill pit

A) $190

B) $1,550

C) $2,800

D) $5,670

Analysis:

unit cost of transport

distance of transport

$$C = R * V * d \leftarrow eq.1$$

total cost $V = A*w$ volume of soil transported

Eq.1 computes the cost of
transporting the soil.

The volume of soil transported
equals the cross-sectional area of
the soil, times the width.

$$C = R * A * w * d \leftarrow eq.2$$

cross-sectional area
of the transported soil   width

Since there is no shrinkage or
swell of the soil, we assume the
area of the pile, A_c, and area of the
pit, A_f, are both equal to the area
of transported soil.

$$A = A_c = -A_f \leftarrow eq.3$$

area of the pile   area of the pit

Subscripts "c" and "f" are used to
represent "cut" and "fill."

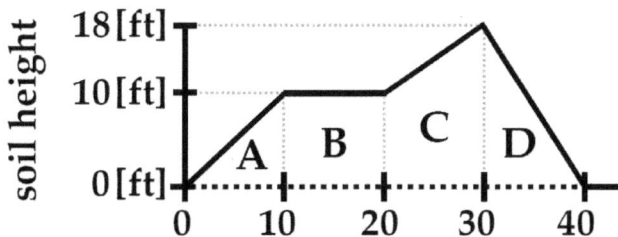

Figure 1 divides the soil pile into 4
distinct areas: A, B, C and D.

Figure 1

Civil Engineering Practice Examination #2

Solution #17 (cont.)

In eq.4, subscript "c" refers to the cut area and subscript "C" refers to area C in Figure 1.

$$A_A = l_A * 0.5 * (h_0 + h_{10})$$

$$A_C = l_C * 0.5 * (h_{20} + h_{30})$$

$$A_c = A_A + A_B + A_C + A_D \quad \leftarrow eq.4$$

$$A_B = l_B * 0.5 * (h_{10} + h_{20})$$

$$A_D = l_D * 0.5 * (h_{30} + h_{40})$$

Eq. 4 computes the cross-sectional area of the soil pile.

Plug in the known length and height values into eq. 5, then solve for A_c.

$$h_0 = 0 \, [ft]$$
$$l_A = 10 \, [ft] \quad h_{10} = 10 \, [ft] \quad l_B = 10 \, [ft] \quad h_{20} = 10 \, [ft]$$

$$A_c = l_A * 0.5 * (h_0 + h_{10}) + l_B * 0.5 * (h_{10} + h_{20})$$

$$+ l_C * 0.5 * (h_{20} + h_{30}) + l_D * 0.5 * (h_{30} + h_{40}) \quad \leftarrow eq.5$$

$$l_C = 10 \, [ft] \quad h_{30} = 18 \, [ft] \quad l_D = 10 \, [ft] \quad h_{40} = 0 \, [ft]$$
$$h_{20} = 10 \, [ft]$$

$$A_c = 10 \, [ft] * 0.5 * (0 \, [ft] + 10 \, [ft]) + 10 \, [ft] * 0.5 * (10 \, [ft] + 10 \, [ft])$$

$$+ 10 \, [ft] * 0.5 * (10 \, [ft] + 18 \, [ft]) + 10 \, [ft] * 0.5 * (18 \, [ft] + 0 \, [ft])$$

$$A_c = 50 \, [ft^2] + 100 \, [ft^2] + 140 \, [ft^2] + 90 \, [ft^2]$$

A_D

$A_A \quad A_B \quad A_C$

$$A_c = 380 \, [ft^2]$$

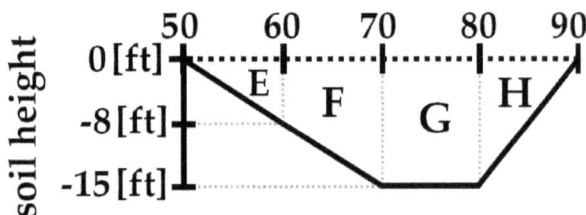

Figure 2

Figure 2 divides the fill pit into 4 distinct areas: E, F, G and H.

$$A_E = l_E * 0.5 * (h_{50} + h_{60})$$

$$A_G = l_G * 0.5 * (h_{70} + h_{80})$$

$$A_f = A_E + A_F + A_G + A_H \quad \leftarrow eq.6$$

$$A_F = l_F * 0.5 * (h_{60} + h_{70})$$

$$A_H = l_H * 0.5 * (h_{80} + h_{90})$$

Eq. 6 computes the cross-sectional area of the fill pit.

Solution #17 (cont.)

Plug in the known length and height values into eq.7, then solve for A_f.

$h_{50}=0\,[ft]$

$l_A=10\,[ft]$ $h_{60}=-8\,[ft]$ $l_F=10\,[ft]$ $h_{70}=-15\,[ft]$

$$A_f=l_E*0.5*(h_{50}+h_{60})+l_F*0.5*(h_{60}+h_{70})$$
$$+l_G*0.5*(h_{70}+h_{80})+l_H*0.5*(h_{80}+h_{90}) \leftarrow eq.7$$

$l_G=10\,[ft]$ $h_{80}=-15\,[ft]$ $l_H=10\,[ft]$ $h_{90}=0\,[ft]$

$h_{70}=-15\,[ft]$

$$A_f=10\,[ft]*0.5*(0\,[ft]+(-8\,[ft]))+10\,[ft]*0.5*((-8\,[ft])+(-15\,[ft]))$$
$$+10\,[ft]*0.5*((-15\,[ft])+(-15\,[ft]))+10\,[ft]*0.5*((-15\,[ft])+(0\,[ft]))$$

$$A_f=-40\,[ft^2]-115\,[ft^2]-150\,[ft^2]-75\,[ft^2]$$

A_E A_F A_G A_H

$$A_f=-380\,[ft^2]$$

$A_c=380\,[ft^2]$ $A_f=-380\,[ft^2]$

As we suspected, the area of the fill equals the area of the pit.

$$A=A_c=-A_f \leftarrow eq.3$$

$$A=380\,[ft^2]=-(-380\,[ft^2])$$

centroid of the pit   centroid of the pile

$$d=\overline{x}_f-\overline{x}_c \leftarrow eq.8$$

Eq.8 computes the distance of transport.

Eq.9 computes the centroid of the pit.

$A_E=-40\,[ft^2]$ $A_F=-115\,[ft^2]$ $x_H=85\,[ft]$

$x_E=55\,[ft]$ $x_F=65\,[ft]$ $x_G=75\,[ft]$ $A_H=-75\,[ft^2]$

$$\overline{x}_f=\frac{x_E*A_E+x_F*A_F+x_G*A_G+x_H*A_H}{A_f} \leftarrow eq.9$$

$A_f=-380\,[ft^2] \rightarrow A_f$ $A_G=-150\,[ft^2]$

In eq.9, x_E, x_F, x_G and x_H represent the distance to the center of areas E, F, G and H.

Solution #17 (cont.)

$$\overline{x}_f = \frac{\begin{array}{c}55\,[ft]*(-40\,[ft^2])+65\,[ft]*(-115[ft^2])\\+75\,[ft]*(-150\,[ft^2])+85\,[ft]*(-75[ft^2])\end{array}}{-380\,[ft^2]}$$

$$\overline{x}_f = 71.84\,[ft]$$

$A_A = 50\,[ft^2]$ $A_B = 100\,[ft^2]$ $x_D = 35\,[ft]$
$x_A = 5\,[ft]$ $x_B = 15\,[ft]$ $x_C = 25\,[ft]$ $A_D = 90\,[ft^2]$

$$\overline{x}_c = \frac{x_A*A_S+x_B*A_B+x_C*A_C+x_D*A_D}{A_c} \leftarrow eq.\,10$$

$A_c = 380\,[ft^2] \rightarrow A_c$ $A_c = 140\,[ft^2]$

Eq. 10 computes the centroid of the pile.

In eq. 10, x_A, x_B, x_C and x_D represent the distance to the center of areas A, B, C and D.

$$\overline{x}_c = \frac{\begin{array}{c}5\,[ft]*50\,[ft^2]+15\,[ft]*100\,[ft^2]\\+25\,[ft]*140\,[ft^2]+35\,[ft]*90\,[ft^2]\end{array}}{380\,[ft^2]}$$

$$\overline{x}_c = 22.11\,[ft]$$

$\overline{x}_f = 71.84\,[ft]$ $\overline{x}_c = 22.11\,[ft]$

$$d = \overline{x}_f - \overline{x}_c \leftarrow eq.\,8$$

Plug in variables $\overline{x}_f$ and $\overline{x}_c$ into eq. 8, then solve for d.

$$d = 71.84\,[ft] - 22.11\,[ft]$$

$$d = 49.73\,[ft]$$

$R = \$0.01\,[ft^{-4}]$ $w = 15\,[ft]$

$$C = R*A*w*d \leftarrow eq.\,2$$

$A = 380\,[ft^2]$ $d = 49.73\,[ft]$

Plug in variables R, A, w and d into eq. 2, then solve for C.

$$C = \$0.01\,[ft^{-4}]*380\,[ft^2]*15\,[ft]*49.73\,[ft]$$

$$C = \$2,835 \qquad \underline{\text{Answer:}} \quad \boxed{C}$$

Solution #18

$E=2.9*10^7[lb/in^2]$
↑
elastic modulus

Find: P_{cr} ← the critical axial force of the column

Given:

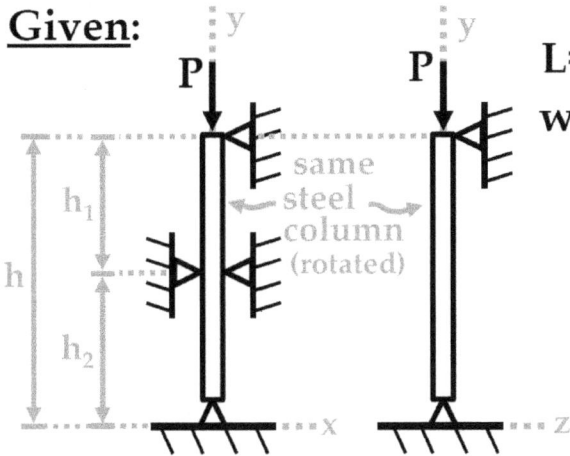

L=2[in] ⎫ the length and width
w=1[in] ⎬ of the steel column

$h_1=10[ft]$

$h_2=12[ft]$

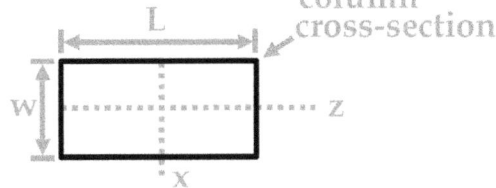

column
cross-section

← all connections are
pin connections

A) 2,300[lb]

B) 2,740[lb]

C) 3,320[lb]

D) 5,480[lb]

Analysis:

critical
force
elastic
modulus
area moment
of inertia

$$P_{cr}=\frac{\pi^2*E*I}{(K*L)^2} \leftarrow eq.1$$

column effective
length factor
unsupported length
of the column

The critical axial force is the
maximum normal force the column
can withstand without buckling.

Eq.1 computes the critical
force of the column.

$$P_{cr}=min(P_{cr,x},P_{cr,z}) \leftarrow eq.2$$

critical force about
the x and z axes

Since the column can buckle about
the x axis or about the z axis, the
critical force will be governed by the
smaller of these two critical forces.

$$P_{cr,z}=\frac{\pi^2*E*I_z}{(K_z*L_z)^2} \leftarrow eq.3$$

Eq.3 computes the critical
force about the z axis.

w=2[in]   L=1[in]

$$I_z=\frac{w*L^3}{12} \leftarrow eq.4$$

Eq.4 computes the area moment of
inertia about the z axis.

$$I_z=\frac{2[in]*(1[in])^3}{12}$$

Plug in variables w and L
into eq.4, then solve for I_z.

$$I_z=0.167[in^4]$$

Civil Engineering Practice Examination #2

Solution #18 (cont.)

$$K_z = 1.00$$

For a pin-pin connection, the column effective length factor equals 1.00.

$$L_z = \max(h_1, h_2) \leftarrow eq.5$$

$h_1 = 10\,[ft] \qquad h_2 = 12\,[ft]$

Since a longer column will result in a lower critical force, the larger of the two column segments is used for the variable L_z.

$$L_z = \max(10\,[ft], 12\,[ft])$$

Plug in h_1 and h_2 into eq.5, then solve for L_z.

$$L_z = 12\,[ft] * 12\left[\frac{in}{ft}\right] \leftarrow eq.6$$

Eq.6 converts L_z to inches by multiplying by 12 inches per foot.

$$L_z = 144\,[in]$$

$E = 2.9*10^7\,[lb/in^2] \qquad I_z = 0.167\,[in^4]$

$$P_{cr,z} = \frac{\pi^2 * E * I_x}{(K_x * L_x)^2} \leftarrow eq.3$$

$K_z = 1.00 \qquad L_z = 144\,[in]$

Plug in variables E, I_z, K_z and I_z into eq.3, then solve for $P_{cr,z}$.

$$P_{cr,z} = \frac{\pi^2 * 2.9*10^7\,[lb/in^2] * 0.167\,[in^4]}{(1.00 * 144\,[in])^2}$$

$$P_{cr,z} = 2{,}305\,[lb]$$

$$P_{cr,x} = \frac{\pi^2 * E * I_x}{(K_x * L_x)^2} \leftarrow eq.7$$

Eq.7 computes the critical force about the x axis.

$w = 1\,[in] \qquad L = 2\,[in]$

$$I_x = \frac{w * L^3}{12} \leftarrow eq.8$$

Eq.8 computes the area moment of inertia about the z axis.

$$I_x = \frac{1\,[in] * (2\,[in])^3}{12}$$

Plug in variables w and L into eq.8, then solve for I_x.

Solution #18 (cont.)

$$I_x = 0.667 [in^4]$$

$$K_x = 1.00$$

The column effective length factor equals 1.00 in the x direction also.

$$L_x = h = h_1 + h_2 \leftarrow eq. 9$$

$$h_1 = 10 [ft] \qquad h_2 = 12 [ft]$$

In the x direction, the unsupported length of the column equals the entire column height, h.

$$L_x = 10 [ft] + 12 [ft]$$

Plug in variables h_1 and h_2 into eq. 9, then solve for L_x.

$$L_x = 22 [ft] * 12 \left[\frac{in}{ft}\right] \leftarrow eq. 10$$

Eq. 10 converts L_z to inches.

$$L_x = 264 [in]$$

$$E = 2.9*10^7 [lb/in^2] \qquad I_z = 0.667 [in^4]$$

$$P_{cr,x} = \frac{\pi^2 * E * I_x}{(K_x * L_x)^2} \leftarrow eq. 7$$

$$K_x = 1.00 \qquad L_x = 264 [in]$$

Plug in variables E, I_z, K_z and I_z into eq. 7, then solve for $P_{cr,z}$.

$$P_{cr,x} = \frac{\pi^2 * 2.9*10^7 [lb/in^2] * 0.667 [in^4]}{(1.00 * 264 [in])^2}$$

$$P_{cr,x} = 2,739 [lb]$$

$$P_{cr} = \min(P_{cr,z}, P_{cr,x}) \leftarrow eq. 2$$

$$P_{cr,z} = 2,305 [lb] \qquad P_{cr,x} = 2,739 [lb]$$

Plug in variables $P_{cr,x}$ and $P_{cr,z}$ into eq. 2, then solve for P_{cr}.

$$P_{cr} = \min(2,305 [lb], 2,739 [lb])$$

$$P_{cr} = 2,305 [lb] \qquad \underline{\textbf{Answer:}} \quad \boxed{A}$$

Civil Engineering Practice Examination #2

Solution #19

Find: I ← the interior angle of the curve

Given:

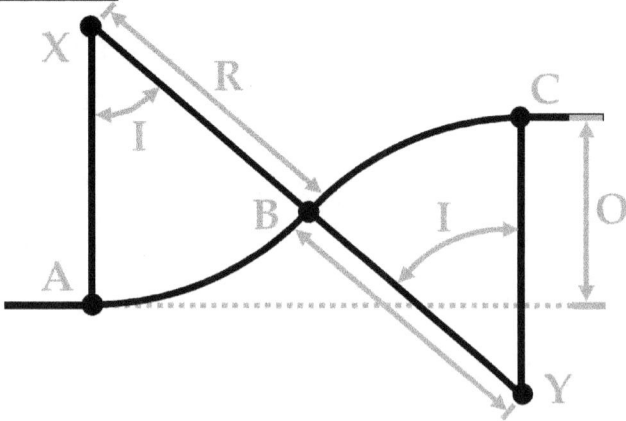

$O = 400\,[\text{ft}]$ ← offset distance

$D = 2.690°$ ← degree of curve [arc-basis]

← the compound horizontal curves share the same interior angle and radius

A) 25°
B) 30°
C) 35°
D) 40°

Analysis:

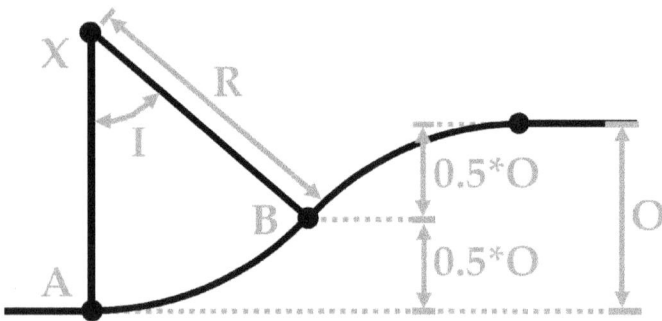

Figure 1

Since both curves share the same radius and interior angle, then point B equally splits the offset distance, and only we need to analyze one curve.

Figure 2 shows how curve AB extends a vertical distance of half the total offset.

Eq. 1 computes half the offset based on the radius and the interior angle.

$$0.5 * O = R - R * \cos(I) \leftarrow eq.\,1$$

Solve eq. 1 for the interior angle.

$$I = \cos^{-1}\left(1 - \frac{0.5 * O}{R}\right) \leftarrow eq.\,2$$

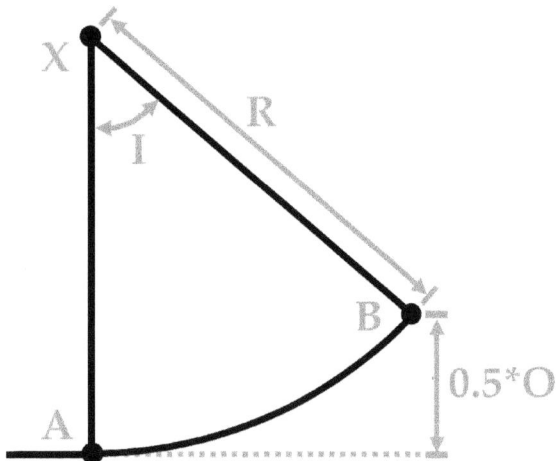

Figure 2

Solution #19 (cont.)

$$D = \frac{360° * 100\,[\text{ft}]}{2 * \pi * R} \leftarrow eq.3$$

radius

Eq.3 computes the degree of the curve (arc-basis).

Solve eq.3 for the radius, R.

$$R = \frac{360° * 100\,[\text{ft}]}{2 * \pi * D} \leftarrow eq.4$$

D = 2.690°

Plug in variable D into eq.4, then solve for R.

$$R = \frac{360° * 100\,[\text{ft}]}{2 * \pi * 2.690°}$$

$$R = 2{,}130\,[\text{ft}]$$

O = 400 [ft]

$$I = \cos^{-1}\left(1 - \frac{0.5 * O}{R}\right) \leftarrow eq.2$$

R = 2,130 [ft]

Plug in variables O and R into eq.2, then solve for I.

$$I = \cos^{-1}\left(1 - \frac{0.5 * 400\,[\text{ft}]}{2{,}130[\text{ft}]}\right)$$

$$I = 25.03°$$

Answer: $\boxed{A}$

Civil Engineering Practice Examination #2

Solution #20

Find: V ← the volume of flow beneath the embankment in a 12 hour period

assume steady-state flow conditions apply

Given:

$L = 20\,[m]$ ← length of the dam and aquifer (into and out of the page)

$t = 12\,[hr]$ ← duration

$K = 0.015\,[cm/s]$ ← hydraulic conductivity

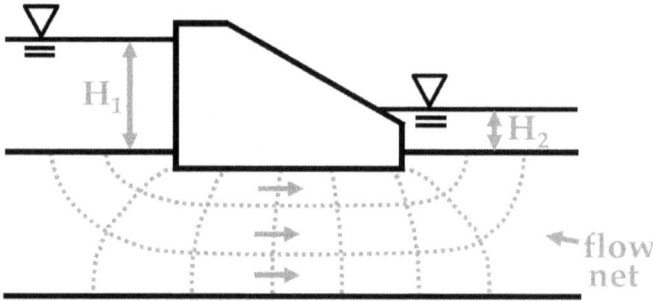

$H_1 = 5.0\,[m]$ upstream head

$H_2 = 1.2\,[m]$ downstream head

← flow net

A) $21\,[m^3]$

B) $250\,[m^3]$

C) $1{,}000\,[m^3]$

D) $25{,}000\,[m^3]$

Analysis:

$$V = Q * t \quad \leftarrow eq.1$$

volume ↗   ↑ flow rate   ↖ time

Eq. 1 computes the volume of water flowing beneath the embankment.

hydraulic conductivity

'flow channels' in the flow net

$$Q = K * \Delta h * \frac{N_F}{N_D} * L \quad \leftarrow eq.2$$

headloss across the embankment

'drops' in the flow net

Eq. 2 computes the flow rate beneath the embankment.

$N_F = 3$

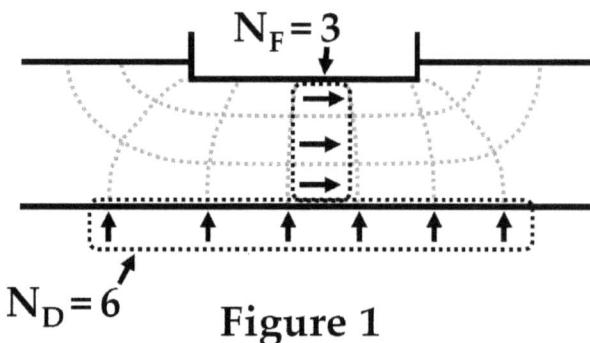

$N_D = 6$

Figure 1

Figure 1 identifies the number of drops and flow channels in the flow net.

$$\Delta h = H_1 - H_2 \quad \leftarrow eq.3$$

$H_1 = 5.0\,[m]$ $H_2 = 1.2\,[m]$

Eq. 3 computes the headloss across the embankment.

Plug in variables H_1 and H_2 into eq. 3, then solve for Δh.

Solution #20 (cont.)

$$\Delta h = 5.0\,[\text{m}] - 1.2\,[\text{m}]$$

$$\Delta h = 3.8\,[\text{m}]$$

$$\underset{\Delta h = 3.8\,[\text{m}]}{\overset{K=0.015\,[\text{cm/s}]}{Q = K * \Delta h *}} \frac{\overset{N_F = 3}{N_F}}{\underset{N_D = 6}{N_D}} * \overset{L=20\,[\text{m}]}{L} \leftarrow eq.\,2$$

Plug in variables K, Δh, N_F, N_D and L into eq. 2, then solve for Q.

$$Q = 0.015\,[\text{cm/s}] * 3.8\,[\text{m}] * \frac{3}{6} * 20\,[\text{m}]$$

Eq. 4 converts the flow rate to units of cubic meters per hour.

$$Q = 0.57 \left[\frac{\text{cm*m}^2}{\text{s}}\right] * \frac{1}{100}\left[\frac{\text{m}}{\text{cm}}\right] * 3{,}600 \left[\frac{\text{s}}{\text{hr}}\right] \leftarrow eq.\,4$$

$$Q = 20.52\,[\text{m}^3/\text{hr}]$$

$$\underset{Q=20.52\,[\text{m}^3/\text{hr}]}{\overset{\text{volume}}{V = Q * t}} \leftarrow eq.\,1 \quad {}_{t=12\,[\text{hr}]}$$

Plug in variables Q and t into eq. 1, then solve for V.

$$V = 20.52\,[\text{m}^3/\text{hr}] * 12\,[\text{hr}]$$

$$V = 246.2\,[\text{m}^3]$$

Answer: $\boxed{\text{B}}$

Civil Engineering Practice Examination #2

Solution #21

Find: i ← the annual interest rate of the investment

Given:

$A_{1\text{-}5}=\$\text{-}15{,}000$ ← the annual deposit at the end of years 1 through 5

$F_{15}=\$135{,}000$ ← the future withdrawal at the end of year 15

A) 4%
B) 5%
C) 6%
D) 7%

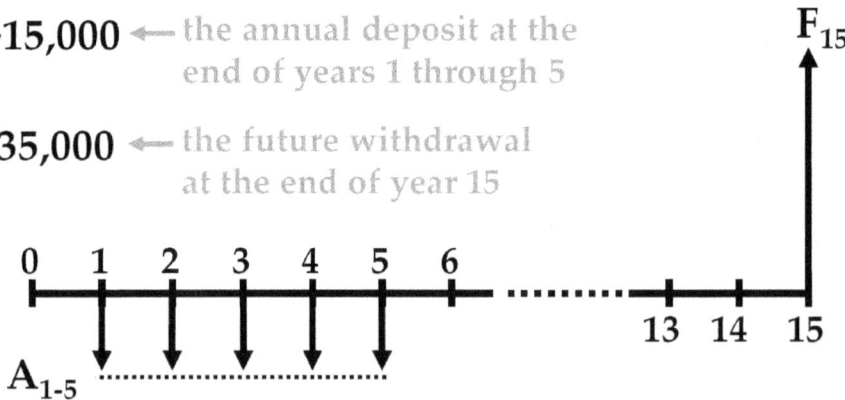

Analysis:

$$P=-A_{1\text{-}5}*(P/A,i,n)=F_{15}*(P/F,i,n) \leftarrow eq.1$$

$A_{1\text{-}5}=\$\text{-}15{,}000$ — uniform series discount factor

$F_{15}=\$135{,}000$ — single payment discount factor

Eq.1 computes the present worth of the investment based on the annual deposit and on the future withdrawal.

Plug in 5 and 15 for the number of years, n, into the two discount factors shown in eq.1.

$$P/A,i,5=\frac{(1+i)^5-1}{i*(1+i)^5} \qquad P/F,i,15=(1+i)^{-15}$$

$$-(-\$15{,}000)*(P/A,i,5)=\$135{,}000*(P/F,i,15) \leftarrow eq.2$$

$$\$15{,}000*\frac{(1+i)^5-1}{i*(1+i)^5}=\$135{,}000*(1+i)^{-15}$$

Plug in the discount factors into eq.2, then simplify.

$$(1+i)^{10}*((1+i)^5-1)/i=9 \leftarrow eq.3$$

Plug in the 4 possible solutions into the left hand side (LHS) of eq.3 and the correct answer will correspond to the LHS closest to 9.

	i	LHS
A	0.04	8.017
B	0.05	9.001
C	0.06	10.095
D	0.07	11.313

Answer: B

Solution #22

<u>Find:</u> P_1 ← the point load acting downward at the end of the circular beam.

<u>Given:</u>

$d=8\,[cm]$ ← the diameter of the beam

$L=31\,[cm]$ ← the length of the beam

$P_2=25\,[N]$ ← the point load acting horizontal at the end of the beam.

$\sigma_A=23{,}470\,[N/m^2]$

the normal stress at point A (in compression)

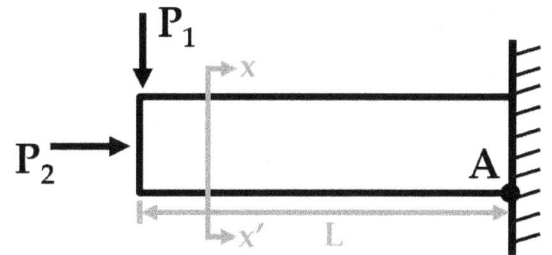

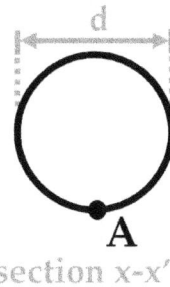

section x-x'

A) 3[N]
B) 6[N]
C) 9[N]
D) 12[N]

Analysis:

normal stress at A

normal force

moment at point A

$$\sigma_A = \frac{P_2}{A} + \frac{M_A * y_A}{I} \leftarrow eq.1$$

cross-sectional area of the beam

area moment of inertia

Eq. 1 computes the normal stress at point A.

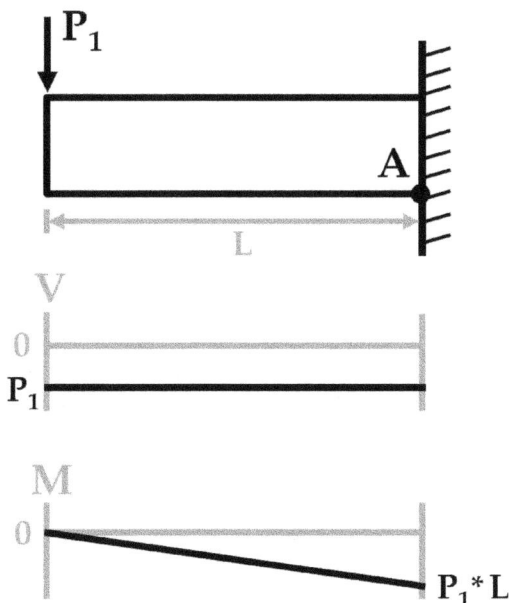

Figure 1

Figure 1 shows the loading diagram, the shear diagram and the moment diagram of the beam.

Point A is located at the bottom of the beam, against the wall.

From the moment diagram we notice the moment at point A equals P_1*L.

Load P_1 creates a compressive stress at point A, so we'll assume moment P_1*L is positive.

vertical point load   beam length

$$M_A = P_1 * L \leftarrow eq.2$$

Eq. 2 computes the moment at point A.

Civil Engineering Practice Examination #2

Solution #22 (cont.)

$$M_A = \underbrace{P_1 * L}_{}$$

$$\sigma_A = \frac{P_2}{A} + \frac{M_A * y_A}{I} \leftarrow eq.1$$

Plug in variable M_A into eq.1, then solve for P_1.

$$\sigma_A = \frac{P_2}{A} + \frac{(P_1 * L) * y_A}{I}$$

$$P_1 = \left(\sigma_A - \frac{P_2}{A}\right) * \left(\frac{I}{L * y_A}\right) \leftarrow eq.3$$

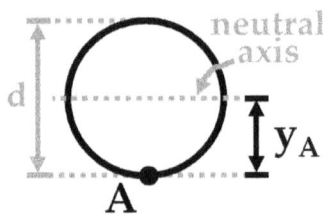

Figure 2

In eq.3, variable y_A refers to the distance between the neutral axis and point A, which equals half the diameter, as shown in Figure 2.

$$d = 8[cm] * \frac{1}{100}\left[\frac{m}{cm}\right] = 0.08[m] \leftarrow eq.4$$

Eq.4 and eq.5 convert the beam diameter and beam length to meters.

$$L = 31[cm] * \frac{1}{100}\left[\frac{m}{cm}\right] = 0.31[m] \leftarrow eq.5$$

$$d = 0.08[m]$$
$$\downarrow$$
$$y_A = d/2 \leftarrow eq.6$$

Eq.6 computes the length y_A. Plug in variable d into eq.6, then solve for y_A.

$$y_A = 0.08[m]/2$$

$$y_A = 0.04[m]$$

$$d = 0.08[m]$$
$$\downarrow$$
$$I = \frac{\pi * d^4}{64} \leftarrow eq.7$$

Eq.7 calculates the area moment of inertia for a circular cross-section.

Plug in the diameter into eq.7, then solve for I.

Solution #22 (cont.)

$$I = \frac{\pi * (0.08\,[m])^4}{64}$$

$$I = 2.011*10^{-6}\,[m^4]$$

$$d = 0.08\,[m]$$

$$A = \frac{\pi * d^2}{4} \leftarrow eq.8$$

Eq. 8 calculates the cross-sectional area of the beam.

Plug in the diameter into eq. 8, then solve for A.

$$A = \frac{\pi * (0.08\,[m])^2}{4}$$

$$A = 5.027*10^{-3}\,[m^2]$$

$$\sigma_A = 23{,}470\,[N/m^2] \qquad I = 2.011*10^{-6}\,[m^4]$$

$$P_1 = \left(\sigma_A - \frac{P_2}{A}\right) * \left(\frac{I}{L * y_A}\right) \leftarrow eq.3$$

$$P_2 = 25\,[N] \qquad L = 0.31\,[m]$$
$$A = 5.027*10^{-3}\,[m^2] \qquad y_A = 0.04\,[m]$$

Plug in variables σ_A, P_2, A, I, L and y_A into eq. 3, then solve for P_1.

$$P_1 = \left(23{,}470\,[N/m^2] - \frac{25\,[N]}{5.027*10^{-3}\,[m^2]}\right) * \left(\frac{2.011*10^{-6}\,[m^4]}{0.31\,[m] * 0.04\,[m]}\right)$$

$$P_1 = 3\,[N]$$

Answer: $\boxed{A}$

Solution #23

<u>Find:</u> **P** ←the pump power

<u>Given:</u>

$d_A = 10$ [in] ← inlet diameter

$d_B = 6$ [in] ← outlet diameter

$P_A = 25$ [lb$_f$/in^2] ← inlet pressure

$P_B = 60$ [lb$_f$/in^2] ← outlet pressure

$Q = 1{,}200$ [gal/min] ← flow rate

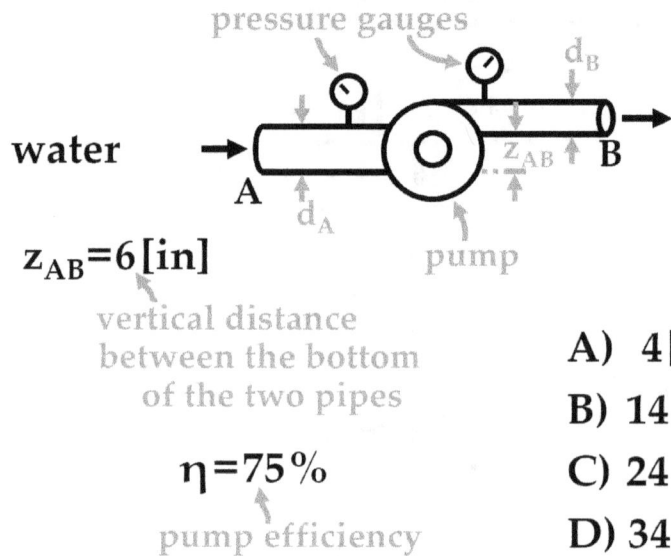

water

$z_{AB} = 6$ [in]

vertical distance between the bottom of the two pipes

$\eta = 75\%$

pump efficiency

pressure gauges

d_B

A d_A

z_{AB} B

pump

A) 4 [hp]
B) 14 [hp]
C) 24 [hp]
D) 34 [hp]

<u>Analysis:</u>

total head added by the pump [ft]   flow rate [gal/min]

$$P = \frac{\Delta h_{AB} * Q * SG}{3{,}956 * \eta} \leftarrow eq.1$$

pump power [hp]   efficiency   specific gravity

Eq. 1 pump power based on the head, flow rate specific gravity and efficiency.

$$\Delta h_{AB} = h_{T,B} - h_{T,A} \leftarrow eq.2$$

total head at points B and A

Eq. 2 computes the total head added by the pump.

$$\Delta h_{AB} = \left(\frac{P_B}{\gamma} + \frac{v_B^2}{2*g} + z_B\right) - \left(\frac{P_A}{\gamma} + \frac{v_A^2}{2*g} + z_A\right) \leftarrow eq.3$$

Eq. 3 writes out the total head terms from eq. 2.

$$\frac{P_B}{\gamma} = 60 \left[\frac{lb_f}{in^2}\right] * \frac{1}{62.4}\left[\frac{ft^3}{lb_f}\right] * \left(12\left[\frac{in}{ft}\right]\right)^2 \leftarrow eq.4$$

unit conversion factor

Eq. 4 computes the pressure head at the outlet.

$$\frac{P_B}{\gamma} = 138.46 \text{ [ft]}$$

flow rate   outlet pipe area

$$v_B = Q/A_B \leftarrow eq.5$$

Eq. 5 computes the water velocity at the outlet.

Solution #23 (cont.)

Eq. 6 converts the flow rate
to cubic feet per second.

$$Q = 1,200 \left[\frac{gal}{min}\right] * \frac{1}{7.48}\left[\frac{ft^3}{gal}\right] * \frac{1}{60}\left[\frac{min}{s}\right] \leftarrow eq.6$$

$$Q = 2.674\,[ft^3/s]$$

area of the
outlet pipe
6 [in]

$$A_B = \frac{\pi * d_B^2}{4} \leftarrow eq.7$$

Eq. 7 computes the area of the outlet
pipe based on the outlet pipe
diameter.

$$A_B = \frac{\pi * (6\,[in])^2}{4}$$

Eq. 8 converts the area of the outlet
pipe to feet squared.

$$A_B = 28.274\,[in^2] * \left(\frac{1}{12}\left[\frac{ft}{in}\right]\right)^2 \leftarrow eq.8$$

$$A_B = 0.1963\,[ft^2]$$

Q=2.674 [ft³/s]

$$v_B = \frac{Q}{A_B} \leftarrow eq.5$$

A_B=0.1963 [ft²]

Plug in variables Q and A_B
into eq. 5, then solve for v_B.

$$v_B = \frac{2.674\,[ft^3/s]}{0.1963\,[ft^2]}$$

$$v_B = 13.62\,[ft/s]$$

$$\frac{P_A}{\gamma} = 25\left[\frac{lb_f}{in^2}\right] * \frac{1}{62.4}\left[\frac{ft^3}{lb_f}\right] * \left(12\left[\frac{in}{ft}\right]\right)^2 \leftarrow eq.9$$

Eq. 9 computes the
pressure head at the inlet.

unit conversion
factor

Solution #23 (cont.)

$$\frac{P_A}{\gamma} = 57.69\,[\text{ft}]$$

$$\underset{\text{flow rate}}{} \quad \underset{\text{inlet pipe area}}{}$$

$$v_A = Q/A_A \leftarrow eq.\,10$$

Eq. 10 computes the water velocity at the inlet.

$$\underset{\substack{\text{area of the} \\ \text{inlet pipe}}}{A_A} = \frac{\pi * d_A^2}{4} \leftarrow eq.\,11 \quad \underset{10\,[\text{in}]}{}$$

Eq. 11 computes the area of the outlet pipe based on the outlet pipe diameter.

$$A_A = \frac{\pi * (10\,[\text{in}])^2}{4}$$

$$A_B = 78.540\,[\text{in}^2] * \left(\frac{1}{12}\left[\frac{\text{ft}}{\text{in}}\right]\right)^2 \leftarrow eq.\,12$$

Eq. 12 converts the area of the outlet pipe to feet squared.

$$A_B = 0.5454\,[\text{ft}^2]$$

$$\underset{Q=2.674\,[\text{ft}^3/\text{s}]}{v_A = \frac{Q}{A_A}} \leftarrow eq.\,10$$
$$\underset{A_A=0.5454\,[\text{ft}^2]}{}$$

Plug in variables Q and A_A into eq. 10, then solve for v_A.

$$v_A = \frac{2.674\,[\text{ft}^3/\text{s}]}{0.5454\,[\text{ft}^2]}$$

$$v_A = 4.903\,[\text{ft/s}]$$

$$z_A = 0\,[\text{in}]$$

Assume the vertical datum is located at the base of the inlet pipe.

$$\underset{z_A=0\,[\text{ft}]}{z_B} = \underset{z_{AB}=0.5\,[\text{ft}]}{z_A + z_{AB}} \leftarrow eq.\,13$$

Eq. 13 computes the elevation head of the outlet pipe.

Solution #23 (cont.)

$$z_B = 0\,[in] + 0.5\,[ft]$$

$$z_B = 0.5\,[in]$$

Plug in the known variables into the right hand side of eq.3, then solve for the total head added by the pump.

$z_B = 0.5\,[ft]$

$\frac{P_A}{\gamma} = 57.69\,[ft]$

$v_B = 13.62\,[ft/s]$

$v_A = 4.903\,[ft/s]$

$$\Delta h_{AB} = \left(\frac{P_B}{\gamma} + \frac{v_B^2}{2*g} + z_B\right) - \left(\frac{P_A}{\gamma} + \frac{v_A^2}{2*g} + z_A\right) \leftarrow eq.3$$

$\frac{P_B}{\gamma} = 138.46\,[ft]$

$g = 32.2\,[ft/s^2]$

$z_A = 0\,[ft]$

$$\Delta h_{AB} = \left(138.46\,[ft] + \frac{(13.62\,[ft/s])^2}{2*32.2\,[ft/s^2]} + 0.5\,[ft]\right)$$

$$- \left(57.69\,[ft] + \frac{(4.903\,[ft/s])^2}{2*32.2\,[ft/s^2]} + 0\,[ft]\right)$$

$$\Delta h_{AB} = 83.78\,[ft]$$

$Q = 1{,}200\,[gal/min]$

$\Delta h_{AB} = 83.78\,[ft]$

$SG = 1.00$

Plug in variables Δh_{AB}, Q, SG and η into eq.1, then solve for P.

$$P = \frac{\Delta h_{AB} * Q * SG}{3{,}956 * \eta} \leftarrow eq.1$$

$\eta = 75\% = 0.75$

For eq.1, the specific gravity of water is 1.00, and convert the efficiency to a decimal.

$$P = \frac{83.78\,[ft] * 1{,}200\,[gal/min] * 1.00}{3{,}956 * 0.75}$$

$$P = 33.88\,[hp]$$

Answer: $\boxed{D}$

Civil Engineering Practice Examination #2

Solution #24

<u>Find</u>: Range of Allowable Water Content

<u>Given:</u>

wc	$\gamma_T [lb/ft^3]$
0.10	114.8
0.15	126.1
0.20	132.6
0.25	136.9
0.30	133.3

← compaction test data

$RC=95\%$

↑ relative compaction

A) 10% - 29%

B) 14% - 25%

C) 17% - 22%

D) 20% - 30%

Analysis:

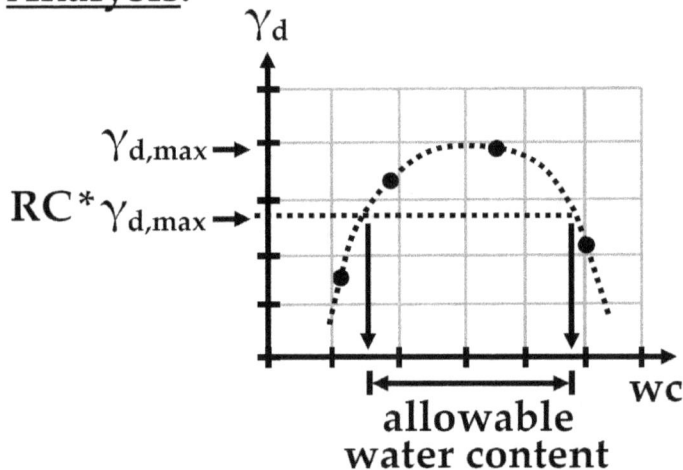

Figure 1

Steps to determine the range of allowable water contents:

i) Plot the wc vs. γ_d for various points
ii) Sketch the compaction curve
iii) Determine the $\gamma_{d,max}$
iv) Compute and sketch $RC^* \gamma_{d,max}$
v) Identify the allowable water content range based on the compaction curve and $RC^* \gamma_{d,max}$

dry unit weight

total unit weight

$$\gamma_d = \frac{\gamma_T}{1+wc} \leftarrow eq.1$$

water content

Eq.1 computes the dry unit weight of a soil sample.

Eq.2 through 6 compute the dry unit weight of the soil, for the 5 samples.

Plug in variables γ_T and wc and compute γ_d, for each sample.

$\gamma_{1,T}=114.8\ [lb/ft^3]$

$$\gamma_{1,d} = \frac{\gamma_{1,T}}{1+wc_1} = \frac{114.8\,[lb/ft^3]}{1+0.10} = 104.4\,[lb/ft^3] \leftarrow eq.2$$

$wc_1=0.10$

Solution #24 (cont.)

$$\gamma_{2,d}=\frac{\gamma_{2,T}}{1+wc_2}=\frac{126.1\,[\text{lb/ft}^3]}{1+0.15}=109.7\,[\text{lb/ft}^3]\ \leftarrow eq.\,3$$

$\gamma_{2,T}=126.1\,[\text{lb/ft}^3]$

$wc_2=0.15$

$$\gamma_{3,d}=\frac{\gamma_{3,T}}{1+wc_3}=\frac{132.6\,[\text{lb/ft}^3]}{1+0.20}=110.5\,[\text{lb/ft}^3]\ \leftarrow eq.\,4$$

$\gamma_{3,T}=132.6\,[\text{lb/ft}^3]$

$wc_3=0.20$

$$\gamma_{4,d}=\frac{\gamma_{4,T}}{1+wc_4}=\frac{136.9\,[\text{lb/ft}^3]}{1+0.25}=109.5\,[\text{lb/ft}^3]\ \leftarrow eq.\,5$$

$\gamma_{4,T}=136.9\,[\text{lb/ft}^3]$

$wc_4=0.25$

$$\gamma_{5,d}=\frac{\gamma_{5,T}}{1+wc_5}=\frac{133.3\,[\text{lb/ft}^3]}{1+0.30}=102.5\,[\text{lb/ft}^3]\ \leftarrow eq.\,6$$

$\gamma_{5,T}=133.3\,[\text{lb/ft}^3]$

$wc_5=0.30$

Plot the 5 data points and sketch the compaction curve

Determine the maximum dry unit weight of the soil.

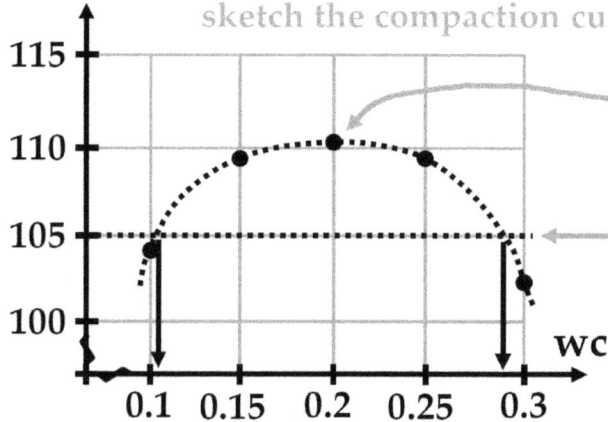

$\gamma_{d,max}=110.5\,[\text{lb/ft}^3]$

Compute and sketch RC* $\gamma_{d,max}$

$0.95*\gamma_{d,max}=0.95*110.5\,[\text{lb/ft}^3]$

$0.95*\gamma_{d,max}=105.0\,[\text{lb/ft}^3]$

Identify the allowable water content range from the plot.

$0.10<wc_{allowable}<0.29$

<u>Answer:</u> A

Civil Engineering Practice Examination #2

Solution #25

Find: d_1 ← the inside diameter of the steel shaft

Given:

$L=1.00\,[\text{m}]$ ← shaft length

$d_2=5\,[\text{cm}]$ ← outer diameter

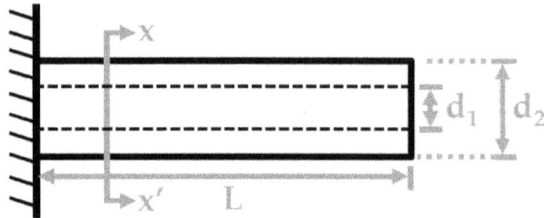

$E=2*10^{11}\,[\text{N/m}^2]$ ← elastic modulus

$T=50\,[\text{N*m}]$ ← applied torque

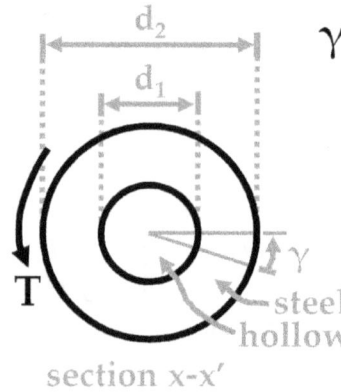

$\gamma=1.06107*10^{-3}\,[\text{rad}]$ ← torsional deflection

$\mathcal{V}=0.30$ ← Poisson's Ratio

A) 1 [cm]

B) 2 [cm]

C) 3 [cm]

D) 4 [cm]

section x-x'
steel hollow

Analysis:

$$J = \frac{\pi*(d_2^4 - d_1^4)}{32} \leftarrow eq.1$$

outside diameter → inside diameter →

Eq. 1 computes the polar moment of inertia for a hollow circular shaft.

$$d_1 = \left(d_2^4 - \frac{32*J}{\pi}\right)^{1/4} \leftarrow eq.2$$

Solve eq. 1 for d_1.

$$\gamma = \frac{T*L}{G*J} \leftarrow eq.3$$

torsion ↗ shaft length ↗
shear modulus ↗   polar moment of inertia ↗

Eq. 3 computes the torsional deflection of the shaft, in radians.

$$J = \frac{T*L}{G*\gamma} \leftarrow eq.4$$

Solve eq. 3 for the polar moment of inertia, J.

$E=2*10^{11}\,[\text{N/m}^2]$

$$G = \frac{E}{2*(1+\mathcal{V})} \leftarrow eq.5$$

$\mathcal{V}=0.30$

Eq. 5 computes the shear modulus of the steel shaft, based on the elastic modulus and Poisson's Ratio.

Plug in variables E and $\mathcal{V}$ into eq. 5 then solve for G.

$$G = \frac{2*10^{11}\,[\text{N/m}^2]}{2*(1+0.30)}$$

Solution #25 (cont.)

$$G = 7.692*10^{10}[N/m^2]$$

T=50[N*m]   L=1.00[m]

$$J = \frac{T*L}{G*\gamma} \leftarrow eq.4$$

$\gamma = 1.06107*10^{-3}$ [rad]

$G = 7.692*10^{10}[N/m^2]$

Plug in variables T, L, G and γ into eq.4, then solve for J.

Drop the units of radians.

$$J = \frac{50[N*m]*1.00[m]}{7.692*10^{10}[N/m^2]*1.06107*10^{-3}[rad]}$$

$$J = 6.126*10^{-7}[m^4]$$

$$d_2 = 5[cm]*\frac{1}{100}\left[\frac{m}{cm}\right] = 0.05[m]$$

Convert the outer diameter to meters.

$d_2 = 0.05$ [m] $J = 6.126*10^{-7}$ [m⁴]

$$d_1 = \left(d_2^4 - \frac{32*J}{\pi}\right)^{1/4} \leftarrow eq.2$$

Plug in variables d_2 and J into eq.2, then solve for d_1.

$$d_1 = \left((0.05[m])^4 - \frac{32*(6.126*10^{-7}[m^4])}{\pi}\right)^{1/4}$$

$$d_1 = 0.01[m]*100\left[\frac{cm}{m}\right] \leftarrow eq.5$$

Eq.5 converts the inner diameter to centimeters.

$$d_1 = 1[cm]$$

Answer: $\boxed{A}$

Civil Engineering Practice Examination #2

Solution #26

Find: L_{AB} ← the length of the vertical curve

Given:

$STA_A = 23+00$ ← the stationing and elevation of point A, the beginning of the vertical curve.

$y_A = 191.58\,[ft]$

the stationing and elevation of point B, the end of the vertical curve.

$STA_B = 26+00$

$y_B = 196.11\,[ft]$

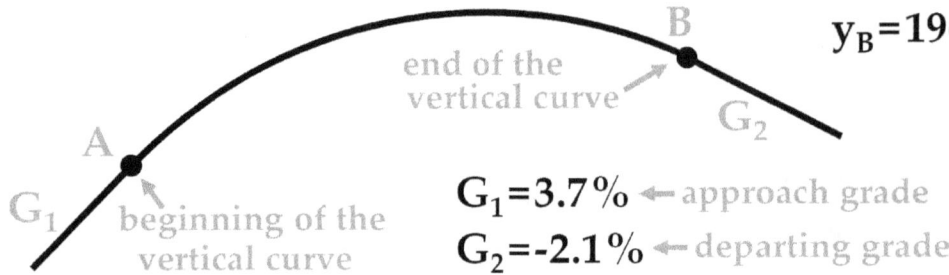

$G_1 = 3.7\%$ ← approach grade

$G_2 = -2.1\%$ ← departing grade

A) 400 [ft]

B) 500 [ft]

C) 600 [ft]

D) 700 [ft]

Analysis:

approach grade   departure grade

$$R = \frac{G_2 - G_1}{L_{AB}} \leftarrow eq.1$$

rate of the grade change   curve length

Eq. 1 calculates the rate of grade change of the vertical curve.

Solve eq.1 for the length of the vertical curve.

$$L_{AB} = \frac{G_2 - G_1}{R} \leftarrow eq.2$$

$$y = 0.5 * R * x^2 + G_1 * x + y_{BVC} \leftarrow eq.3$$

Eq. 3 defines a vertical curve. We'll use eq. 3 to find R.

$$y_B = 0.5 * R * L_{AB}^2 + G_1 * L_{AB} + y_A \leftarrow eq.4$$

Modify eq.3 to fit this problem with point A and point B.

$STA_B = 26+00 = 2,600\,[ft]$

$$L_{AB} = STA_B - STA_A \leftarrow eq.5$$

$STA_A = 23+00 = 2,300\,[ft]$

Eq. 5 computes L_{AB}, the horizontal distance between points A and B.

$$L_{AB} = 2,600\,[ft] - 2,300\,[ft]$$

Plug in variables STA_B and STA_A into eq.5, then solve for L_{AB}.

$$L_{AB} = 300\,[ft]$$

Solution #26 (cont.)

$L_{AB} = 300 \, [ft]$ $y_A = 191.58 \, [ft]$

$$y_B = 0.5 * R * L_{AB}^2 + G_1 * L_{AB} + y_A \leftarrow eq.4$$

Plug in variables y_B, L_{AB}, G_1 and y_A into eq. 4, then solve for R.

$y_B = 196.11 \, [ft]$ $G_1 = 3.7\% = 0.037$

$$196.11 \, [ft] = 0.5 * R * (300 \, [ft])^2 + 0.037 * 300 \, [ft] + 191.58 \, [ft]$$

$$R = -1.46 * 10^{-4} \, [ft^{-1}]$$

Plug in variables y_p, x_p, G_1 and y_{BVC} into eq. 4, then solve for eq. 4.

$G_2 = -2.1\% = -0.021$ $G_1 = 3.7\% = 0.037$

$$L = \frac{G_2 - G_1}{R} \leftarrow eq.2$$

$R = -1.46 * 10^{-4} \, [ft^{-1}]$

$$L = \frac{-0.021 - 0.037}{-1.46 * 10^{-4} \, [ft^{-1}]}$$

$$L = 397.3 \, [ft]$$

Answer: $\boxed{A}$

Civil Engineering Practice Examination #2

Solution #27

Find: T ← the number of truck loads required to remove the excess soil after the terrain elevation is leveled to elevation equals 0 feet

Given:

$w = 20\,[ft]$ ← width of cut pile and fill pit (into and out of the page)

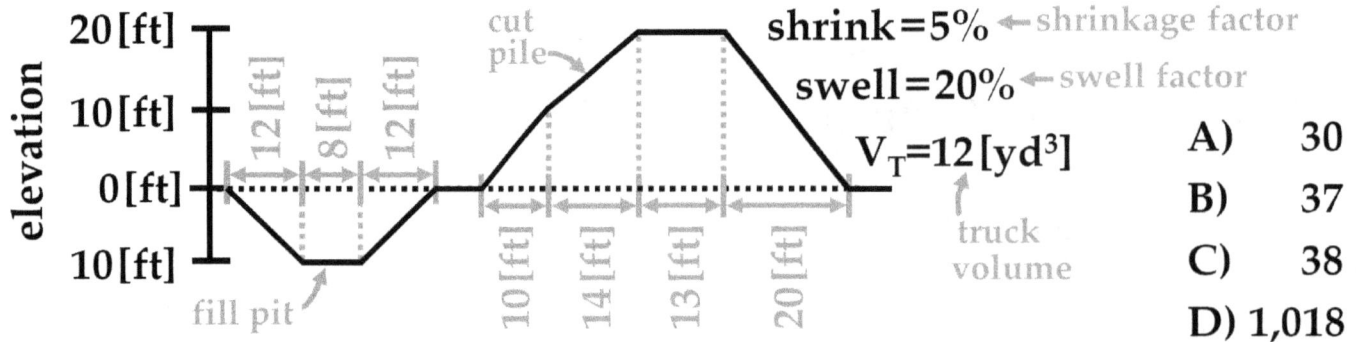

shrink = 5% ← shrinkage factor

swell = 20% ← swell factor

$V_T = 12\,[yd^3]$ ← truck volume

A) 30
B) 37
C) 38
D) 1,018

Analysis:

Eq. 1 computes the number of truck loads required to remove the excess soil.

$$T = \frac{V_{excess}}{V_T} \leftarrow eq.1$$

(V_excess = volume of excess soil after cutting and filling; V_T = truck volume)

Eq. 2 computes the volume of excess soil after cutting and filling.

$$V_{excess} = \left(V_{cut} - \left(\frac{V_{fill}}{1-shrink} \right) \right) * (1+swell) \leftarrow eq.2$$

(volume of cut pile; volume of fill pit; shrinkage factor; swell factor)

Eq. 2 assumes the volume of the cut pile is sufficient to fill the pit.

$$V_{cut} = w * A_{cut} \leftarrow eq.3$$

(constant width of the cut pile; cross-sectional area of the cut pile)

Eq. 3 computes the volume of the cut pile.

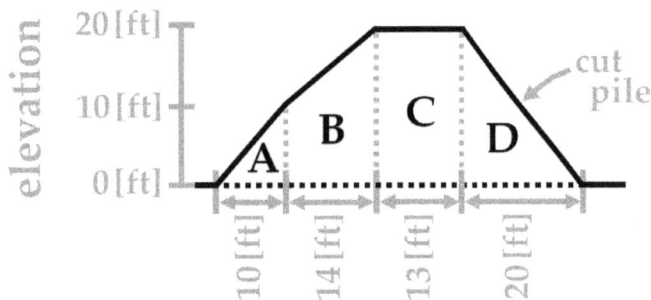

Figure 1 shows the cross-sectional area of the pile, divided into 4 separate areas, A, B, C and D.

Figure 1

Solution #27 (cont.)

$$A_A=10[ft]*0.5*(0[ft]+10[ft])$$

$$A_C=13[ft]*20[ft]$$

$$A_{cut}=A_A+A_B+A_C+A_D \quad \leftarrow eq.4$$

$$A_D=20[ft]*0.5*(0[ft]+20[ft])$$

$$A_B=14[ft]*10[ft]+14[ft]*0.5*(0[ft]+10[ft])$$

Eq. 4 computes the area of the cut pile.

Plug in the equations for A_A, A_B, A_C and A_D, then solve for A_{cut}.

$$A_{cut}= 10[ft]*0.5*(0[ft]+10[ft])$$
$$+14[ft]*10[ft]+14[ft]*0.5*(0[ft]+10[ft])$$
$$+13[ft]*20[ft]$$
$$+20[ft]*0.5*(0[ft]+20[ft])$$

$$A_{cut}=720[ft^2]$$

Areas A, B, C and D are triangular, trapezoidal, and rectangular shaped.

$$w=20[ft] \qquad A_{cut}=720[ft^2]$$

$$V_{cut}=w*A_{cut} \quad \leftarrow eq.3$$

Plug in variables w and A_{cut} into eq. 3, then solve for V_{cut}.

$$V_{cut}=20[ft]*720[ft^2]$$

$$V_{cut}=14,400[ft^3]$$

constant width of the cut pile

cross-sectional area of the cut pile

$$V_{fill}=w*A_{fill} \quad \leftarrow eq.5$$

Eq. 5 computes the volume of the fill pit.

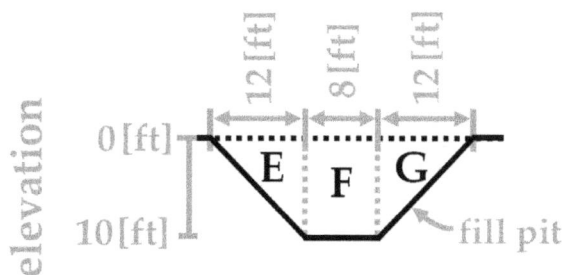

elevation

Figure 2 shows the cross-sectional area of the fill pit, divided into 3 separate areas, E, F and G.

Figure 2

Civil Engineering Practice Examination #2

Solution #27 (cont.)

$A_E = 12\,[ft]*0.5*(0\,[ft]+10\,[ft])$

$A_F = 8\,[ft]*10[ft]$

Eq. 6 computes the area of the fill pit.

$$A_{fill}=A_E+A_F+A_G \leftarrow eq.6$$

Plug in the equations for A_E, A_F and A_G, then solve for A_{fill}.

$A_G = 12\,[ft]*0.5*(0\,[ft]+10\,[ft])$

$$A_{fill}=12\,[ft]*0.5*(0\,[ft]+10\,[ft])+8\,[ft]*10\,[ft]+12\,[ft]*0.5*(0\,[ft]+10\,[ft])$$

$$A_{fill}=200\,[ft^2]$$

$w=20\,[ft]$ $A_{fill}=200\,[ft^2]$

$$V_{fill}=w*A_{fill} \leftarrow eq.5$$

Plug in variables w and A_{fill} into eq.5, then solve for V_{fill}.

$$V_{fill}=20\,[ft]*200\,[ft^2]$$

$$V_{fill}=4,000\,[ft^3]$$

Plug in variables V_{cut}, V_{fill}, shrink and swell into eq.2, then solve for V_{excess}.

$V_{cut}=14,400\,[ft^3]$ $V_{fill}=4,000\,[ft^3]$

$$V_{excess}=\left(V_{cut}-\left(\frac{V_{fill}}{1-shrink}\right)\right)*(1+swell) \leftarrow eq.2$$

shrink$=5\%=0.05$ swell$=20\%=0.20$

$$V_{excess}=\left(14,400\,[ft^3]-\left(\frac{4,000\,[ft^3]}{1-0.05}\right)\right)*(1+0.20)$$

$$V_{excess}=12,227\,[ft^3]*\frac{1}{27}\left[\frac{yd^3}{ft^3}\right]$$

Convert the excess volume from cubic feet to cubic yards.

$$V_{excess}=452.9\,[yd^3]$$

Solution #27 (cont.)

$V_{excess}=452.9\,[yd^3]$

$$T = \frac{V_{excess}}{V_T} \leftarrow eq.1$$

$V_T=12\,[yd^3/truck\ load]$

Plug in variables V_{excess} and V_T into eq. 1, then solve for T

$$T = \frac{452.9\,[yd^3]}{12\,[yd^3\,/\,truck\ load]}$$

T=37.7 truck loads

Round the calculated number of trips up to the nearest integer.

T=38 truck loads

Answer: $\boxed{C}$

Civil Engineering Practice Examination #2

Solution #28

<u>Find:</u> $BOD_{5,30°C}$ ←the biochemical oxygen demand after 5 days at a temperature of 30°C.

<u>Given:</u>

$BOD_{5,20°C}=210\,[mg/L]$ ←the biochemical oxygen demand after 5 days at a temperature of 20°C.

$K_{d,20°C}=0.23\,[day^{-1}]$

deoxygenation rate constant at 20°C.

$\theta=1.047$ ←temperature constant

A) 159 [mg/L]

B) 223 [mg/L]

C) 258 [mg/L]

D) 307 [mg/L]

Analysis:

ultimate BOD   rate of deoxygenation

$$BOD_{5,30°C}=BOD_U*(1-e^{-K_{d,30°C}*t}) \leftarrow eq.1$$

5-day BOD at 30°C   time

Eq. 1 computes the 5-day BOD at 30°C.

$$BOD_{5,20°C}=BOD_U*(1-e^{-K_{d,20°C}*t}) \leftarrow eq.2$$

5-day BOD at 20°C

Eq. 2 computes the 5-day BOD at 20°C.

$BOD_{5,20°C}=210\,[mg/L]$

$$BOD_U=\frac{BOD_{5,20°C}}{1-e^{-K_{d,20°C}*t}} \leftarrow eq.3$$

$t=5\,[days]$

$K_{d,20°C}=0.23\,[day^{-1}]$

Solve eq.2 for the ultimate BOD.

Plug in variables $BOD_{5,20°C}$, $K_{d,20°C}$, and t into eq.3, then solve for BOD_U.

$$BOD_U=\frac{210\,[mg/L]}{1-e^{-0.23[day^{-1}]*5[days]}}$$

$$BOD_U=307.3\,[mg/L]$$

Solution #28 (cont.)

Eq.4 converts the deoxygenation rate between temperatures T_1 and T_2 based on the temperature constant, θ.

$T_1=20°C$

$$K_{d,T_2}=K_{d,T_1}*\theta^{T_2-T_1} \leftarrow eq.4$$

$T_2=30°C$

Plug in 30°C for T_2 and 20°C for T_1 in eq.4.

$\theta=1.047$

$$K_{d,30°C}=K_{d,20°C}*\theta^{30-20} \leftarrow eq.5$$

$K_{d,20°C}=0.23[day^{-1}]$

Plug in $K_{d,20°C}$ and θ into eq.5, then solve for $K_{d,30°C}$.

$$K_{d,30°C}=0.23[day^{-1}]*1.047^{10}$$

$$K_{d,30°C}=0.364[day^{-1}]$$

$K_{d,30°C}=0.364[day^{-1}]$

Plug in $K_{d,30°C}$, t, and BOD_U eq.1, then solve for $BOD_{5,30°C}$.

$$BOD_{5,30°C}=BOD_U*(1-e^{-K_{d,30°C}*t}) \leftarrow eq.1$$

$BOD_U=307.3[mg/L]$ $t=5[days]$

$$BOD_{5,30°C}=307.3[mg/L]*(1-e^{-0.364[day^{-1}]*5[day]})$$

$$BOD_{5,30°C}=257.5[mg/L]$$

Answer: $\boxed{C}$

Civil Engineering Practice Examination #2

Solution #29

Find: $LL_{B,max}$ ← the maximum live load at point B

Given:

$DL_{AC}=2,000 [lb/ft]$ ← the dead load from point A to point C

$y_{max}=0.040 [in]$ ← maximum deflection in the beam

$E=2.9*10^7 [lb/in^2]$
elastic modulus

$I=1,650 [in^4]$
area moment of inertia

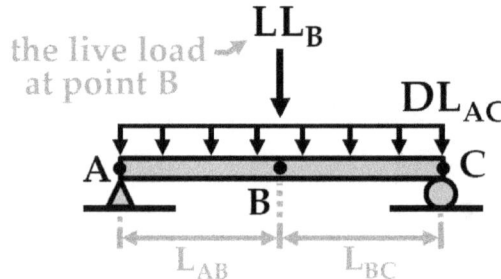

$L_{AB}=6 [ft]$ ⎫ length along
$L_{BC}=6 [ft]$ ⎭ the beam

the live load → LL_B
at point B

DL_{AC}

A ▲——B——○ C

used load factors

A) 7,980 [lb]

B) 9,770 [lb]

C) 12,770 [lb]

D) 21,000 [lb]

L_{AB} L_{BC}

Analysis:

$$y_{max}= \boxed{\frac{P*L^3}{48*E*I}} + \boxed{\frac{5*w*L^4}{384*E*I}} \leftarrow eq.1$$

deflection from the point load   deflection from the uniform load

Eq. 1 computes the maximum deflection, which occurs at the mid-span of the simply-supported beam

The point load and uniform load both contribute to the maximum deflection in the beam.

$$P = \frac{48*E*I*y_{max}}{L^3} - \frac{240*w*L}{384} \leftarrow eq.2$$

Solve eq. 1 for the point load, P, because the live load is a function of the point load.

$L_{AB}=6 [ft]$ $L_{BC}=6 [ft]$

$$L=L_{AB}+L_{BC} \leftarrow eq.3$$

$$L=6 [ft]+6 [ft]$$

$$L=12 [ft]$$

Eq. 3 computes the total length of the beam, L. Plug in variables L_{AB} and L_{AC} into eq. 3, then solve for L.

$E=2.9*10^7 [lb/in^2]$ $y_{max}=0.040 [in]$

$$P= \frac{48*E*I*y_{max}}{L^3} - \frac{240*w*L}{384} \leftarrow eq.2$$

$I=1,650 [in^4]$ $L=12 [ft]$

Plug in variables E, I, y_{max}, and L into eq. 2, then simplify.

96

Solution #29 (cont.)

$$P = \frac{48 * 2.9 * 10^7 [lb/in^2] * 1,650 [in^4] * 0.040 [in]}{(12 [ft])^3} - \frac{240 * w * 12 [ft]}{384}$$

$$P = 5.317 * 10^7 \left[\frac{lb * in^3}{ft^3}\right] * \left(\frac{1}{12}\left[\frac{ft}{in}\right]\right)^3 - 7.5 * w [ft] \leftarrow eq.4$$

unit conversion
factor

Convert the units of the first term on the right hand side of eq.4 to pounds by multiplying by a unit conversion factor.

$$P = 30,770 [lb] - 7.5 [ft] * w \leftarrow eq.5$$

Since 0.04 inches is the maximum deflection in the beam, we want to identify the load factor combination which produces this deflection and then back-calculate the live load at point B.

$$LL_{B,max} = min(LL_{B,I}, LL_{B,II}) \leftarrow eq.6$$

load combinations I and II

The governing load factor combo will be the combination where the smallest live load produces a deflection of 0.04 inches in the beam.

Load Combo I → $U = 1.4 * DL \leftarrow eq.7$

$DL_{AC} = 2,000 [lb/ft]$

$$w_I = 1.4 * DL_{AC} \leftarrow eq.8$$

$$w_I = 1.4 * 2,000 [lb/ft]$$

$$w_I = 2,800 [lb/ft]$$

Eq.8 computes the factored uniform load for load combination I. Plug in DL_{AC} into eq.8, then solve for w.

The subscript "I" refers to load combination I.

$$P_I = 1.0 * LL_{B,I} \leftarrow eq.9$$

$$P_I = LL_{B,I}$$

Eq.9 computes the factored point load for load combination I.

$P_I = LL_{B,I}$ $w_I = 2,800 [lb/ft]$

$$P_I = 30,770 [lb] - 7.5 [ft] * w_I \leftarrow eq.5$$

Plug in variables P_I and w_I into eq.5 for load combination I, then solve for $LL_{B,I}$.

Solution #29 (cont.)

$$LL_{B,I}=30,770\,[lb]-7.5\,[ft]*2,800\,[lb/ft]$$

$$LL_{B,I}=9,770\,[lb]$$

Load Combo II → $U=1.2*DL+1.6*DL$ ←eq. 10

$DL_{AC}=2,000\,[lb/ft]$

$$w_{II}=1.2*DL_{AC} \quad ←eq.11$$

$$w_{II}=1.2*2,000\,[lb/ft]$$

$$w_{II}=2,400\,[lb/ft]$$

Eq. 11 computes the factored uniform load for load combo II. Plug in DL_{AC} into eq. 11, then solve for w_{II}.

The subscript "II" refers to load combination II.

$$P_{II}=1.6*LL_B \quad ←eq.12$$

Eq. 12 computes the factored point load for load combination II.

$P_{II}=1.6*LL_{B,II}$ $w_{II}=2,400\,[lb/ft]$

$$P_{II}=30,770\,[lb]-7.5\,[ft]*w_{II} \quad ←eq.5$$

Plug in variables P_{II} and w_{II} into eq. 5 for load combination II, then solve for $LL_{B,II}$.

$$1.6*LL_{B,II}=30,770\,[lb]-7.5\,[ft]*2,400\,[lb/ft]$$

$$LL_{B,max}=7,981\,[lb]$$

Plug in variables $LL_{B,I}$ and $LL_{B,II}$ into eq. 6, then solve for $LL_{B,max}$.

$$LL_{B,max}=min\,(LL_{B,I}, LL_{B,II}) \quad ←eq.6$$

$LL_{B,I}=9,770\,[lb]$ $LL_{B,II}=7,981\,[lb]$

$$LL_{B,max}=min\,(9,770\,[lb],\ 7,981\,[lb])$$

$$LL_{B,max}=7,981\,[lb]$$

Answer: $\boxed{A}$

Solution #30

Find: C_{AB} ← the major cord from A to B of the horizontal curve

Given:

$v_A = 3.4\,[\text{mi/hr}]$ ← the velocity of the vehicle at points A and B

$v_B = 33.7\,[\text{mi/hr}]$

$I = 120°$ ← interior angle

$a_{AB} = 1\,[\text{ft/s}^2]$ ← constant acceleration of the vehicle between points A and B

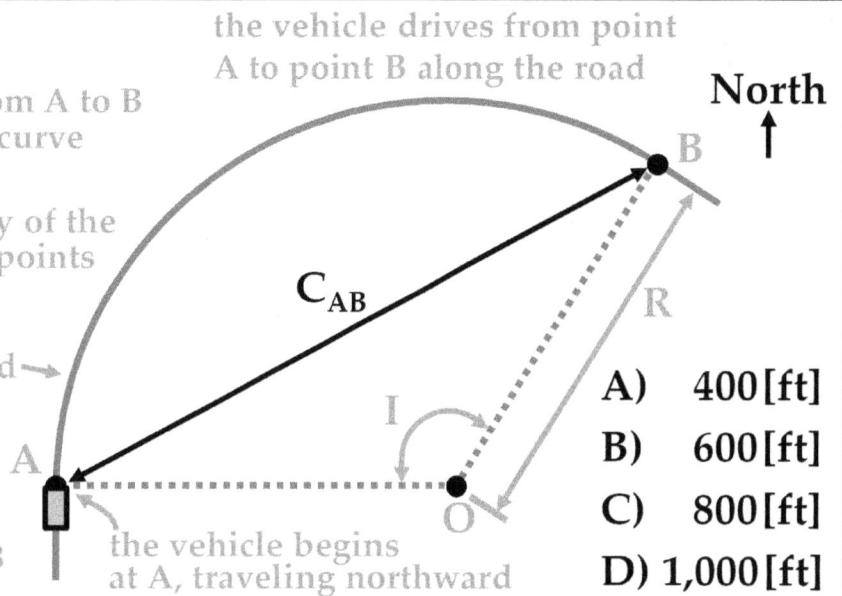

the vehicle drives from point A to point B along the road

North ↑

road →

C_{AB}

R

I

A O

the vehicle begins at A, traveling northward

A)   400 [ft]

B)   600 [ft]

C)   800 [ft]

D) 1,000 [ft]

Analysis:

radius   *interior angle*

$$C_{AB} = 2 * R * \sin(I/2) \leftarrow eq.1$$

chord length

Eq.1 computes the chord length of the horizontal curve from point A to point B.

curve length →

$$L_{AB} = \frac{2 * \pi * R * I}{360°} \leftarrow eq.2$$

Eq.2 computes the length of curve from point A to point B.

$$R = \frac{360° * L_{AB}}{2 * \pi * I} \leftarrow eq.3$$

Solve eq.2 for the radius, R.

velocities at points B and A

$$L_{AB} = \frac{v_B^2 - v_A^2}{2 * a_{AB}} \leftarrow eq.4$$

acceleration

Eq.4 computes the length along the curve based on the acceleration and velocities.

Eq.5 and eq.6 convert the velocities to feet per second.

$$v_B = 33.7\left[\frac{\text{mi}}{\text{hr}}\right] * 5,280\left[\frac{\text{ft}}{\text{mi}}\right] * \frac{1}{3,600}\left[\frac{\text{hr}}{\text{s}}\right] \leftarrow eq.5 \qquad v_B = 49.43\left[\frac{\text{ft}}{\text{s}}\right]$$

$$v_A = 3.4\left[\frac{\text{mi}}{\text{hr}}\right] * 5,280\left[\frac{\text{ft}}{\text{mi}}\right] * \frac{1}{3,600}\left[\frac{\text{hr}}{\text{s}}\right] \leftarrow eq.6 \qquad v_A = 4.99\left[\frac{\text{ft}}{\text{s}}\right]$$

Civil Engineering Practice Examination #2

Solution #30 (cont.)

$v_B = 49.43\,[\text{ft/s}]$ $v_A = 4.99\,[\text{ft/s}]$

$$L_{AB} = \frac{v_B{}^2 - v_A{}^2}{2 * a_{AB}} \leftarrow eq.4$$

$a_{AB} = 1\,[\text{ft/s}^2]$

Plug in variables v_B, v_A and a into eq. 4, then solve for L_{AB}.

$$L_{AB} = \frac{(49.43\,[\text{ft/s}])^2 - (4.99\,[\text{ft/s}])^2}{2 * 1\,[\text{ft/s}^2]}$$

$$L_{AB} = 1{,}209\,[\text{ft}]$$

$L_{AB} = 1{,}209\,[\text{ft}]$

$$R = \frac{360° * L_{AB}}{2 * \pi * I} \leftarrow eq.3$$

$I = 120°$

Plug in variables L_{AB} and I into eq. 3, then solve for R.

$$R = \frac{360° * 1{,}209\,[\text{ft}]}{2 * \pi * 120°}$$

$$R = 577.3\,[\text{ft}]$$

$R = 577.3\,[\text{ft}]$ $I = 120°$

$$C_{AB} = 2 * R * \sin(I/2) \leftarrow eq.1$$

Plug in variables R and I into eq. 1, then solve for C_{AB}.

$$C_{AB} = 2 * 577.3\,[\text{ft}] * \sin(120°/2)$$

$$C_{AB} = 999.9\,[\text{ft}]$$

Answer: $\boxed{D}$

Solution #31

<u>Find:</u> ϱ_c ← ultimate consolidation
settlement of the clay layer

<u>Given:</u>

groundwater table is at
the sand-clay interface

$\Delta\sigma=300\,[lb/ft^2]$ ← loading

sand

10 [ft]

$\gamma'=110\,[lb/ft^3]$ ← effective unit weight
of the sand layer

clay is normally
consolidated

clay

10 [ft]

properties of → the clay layer

$$\begin{bmatrix} wc=25\% \leftarrow \text{water content} \\ SG=2.65 \leftarrow \text{specific gravity} \\ C_C=0.70 \leftarrow \text{consolidation index} \end{bmatrix}$$

rock

A) 0.11 [ft]

B) 0.21 [ft]

C) 0.29 [ft]

D) 0.35 [ft]

Analysis:

layer thickness   compression index   loading

$$\varrho_c = \frac{H*C_C}{1+e_o} * \log\left(\frac{\sigma_v'+\Delta\sigma}{\sigma_v'}\right) \leftarrow eq.1$$

initial void ratio   initial vertical effective stress at the middle of the consolidating layer

Eq.1 computes the consolidation
settlement for a normally
consolidated soil layer.

saturation   water content   specific gravity

$$S = \frac{wc*SG}{e} \leftarrow eq.2$$

void ratio

Eq.2 computes the saturation.

Solve eq.2 for the void ratio.

$wc=25\%=0.25$ $SG=2.65$

$$e_o = e = \frac{wc*SG}{S} \leftarrow eq.3$$

$S=1$

Plug in variables wc, SG and S
into eq.3, then solve for the initial
void ratio of the clay layer.

In eq.3, S=1 because the clay is
beneath the groundwater table.

$$e_o = \frac{0.25*2.65}{1} = 0.663$$

Eq.4 computes the initial vertical
effective stress at the middle of the
clay layer.

effective unit weight of the soil

$$\sigma_v' = \sigma_v'_{@\ d=15[ft]} = \gamma'_{sand}*d_{sand} + \gamma'_{clay}*0.5*d_{clay} \leftarrow eq.4$$

thickness of the soil layer

Civil Engineering Practice Examination #2

Solution #31 (cont.)

$$\gamma'_{clay} = \gamma_{clay} - \gamma_w \leftarrow eq.5$$

Eq. 5 computes the effective unit weight of the clay layer.

$$SG = 2.65 \qquad \gamma_W = 62.4 \ [lb/ft^3]$$

$$\gamma_{clay} = \gamma_{clay,sat} = \frac{(SG + e) * \gamma_W}{1 + e} \leftarrow eq.6$$

$$e_o = e = 0.663$$

Eq. 6 computes the total unit weight of the clay layer under saturated conditions.

$$\gamma_{clay} = \frac{(2.65 + 0.663) * 62.4 \ [lb/ft^3]}{1 + 0.663}$$

Plug in variables SG, γ_W and e_o into eq. 6, then solve for γ_{clay}.

$$\gamma_{clay} = 124.3 \ [lb/ft^3]$$

$$\gamma_{clay} = 124.3 \ [lb/ft^3] \qquad \gamma_W = 62.4 \ [lb/ft^3]$$

$$\gamma'_{clay} = \gamma_{clay} - \gamma_w \leftarrow eq.5$$

Plug in variables γ_{clay} and γ_W into eq. 5, then solve for γ'_{clay}.

$$\gamma'_{clay} = 124.3 \ [lb/ft^3] - 62.4 \ [lb/ft^3]$$

$$\gamma'_{clay} = 61.9 \ [lb/ft^3]$$

Plug in variables γ'_{sand}, d_{sand}, γ'_{clay} and d_{clay} into eq. 4, then solve for σ_v'.

$$\gamma'_{sand} = 110 \ [lb/ft^3] \qquad \gamma'_{clay} = 61.9 \ [lb/ft^3]$$

$$\sigma_v' = \gamma'_{sand} * d_{sand} + \gamma'_{clay} * 0.5 * d_{clay} \leftarrow eq.4$$

$$d_{sand} = 10 \ [ft] \qquad d_{clay} = 10 \ [ft]$$

$$\sigma_v' = 110 \ [lb/ft^3] * 10 \ [ft] + 61.9 \ [lb/ft^3] * 0.5 * 10 \ [ft]$$

$$\sigma_v' = 1,410 \ [lb/ft^2]$$

$$H = 10 \ [ft] \qquad C_C = 0.70 \qquad \Delta\sigma = 300 \ [lb/ft^2]$$

$$Q_c = \frac{H * C_C}{1 + e_o} * \log\left(\frac{\sigma_v' + \Delta\sigma}{\sigma_v'}\right) \leftarrow eq.1$$

Plug in the known variables into eq. 1, then solve for Q_c.

$$e_o = 0.663 \qquad \sigma_v' = 1,410 \ [lb/ft^2]$$

Solution #31 (cont.)

$$\varrho_c = \frac{10[\text{ft}] * 0.70}{1+0.663} * \log\left(\frac{1{,}410[\text{lb/ft}^2]+300[\text{lb/ft}^2]}{1{,}410[\text{lb/ft}^2]}\right)$$

$$\varrho_c = 0.353[\text{ft}]$$

Answer: $\boxed{\text{C}}$

Civil Engineering Practice Examination #2

Solution #32

Find: N ←the minimum number of staff needed to meet the work demand

Given:

all staff are scheduled to work for two consecutive 4-hour shifts, in a 24-hour time period.

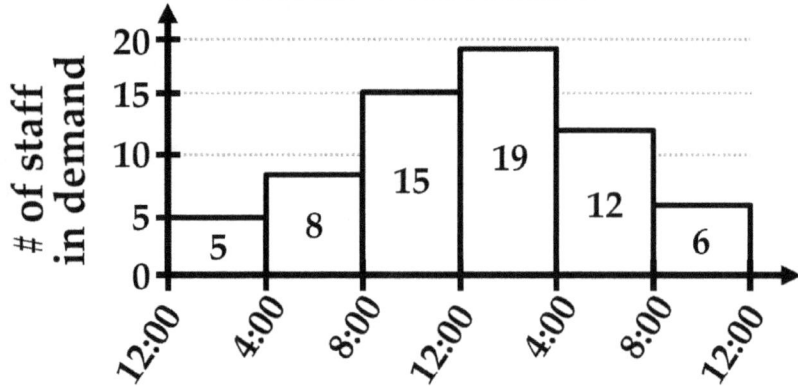

staff can work the shift from 8:00 pm-4:00 am.

$$w_i \geq d_i$$

number of workers must meet or exceed the work demand for all 6 shifts

A) 32

B) 33

C) 34

D) 35

Analysis:

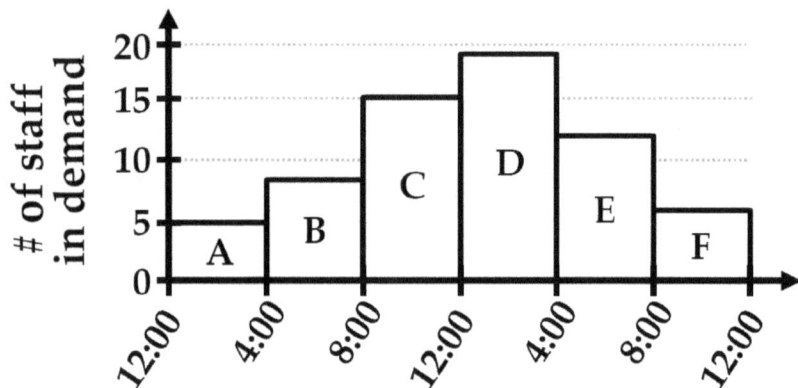

Identify the 6 shifts using letters A, B, C, D, E and F.

Identify the work demands for each shift.

$d_A=5 \qquad d_C=15 \qquad d_E=12$

$d_B=8 \qquad d_D=19 \qquad d_F=6$

Define x_i as the number of staff who begin work on shift i.

$$N = x_A + x_B + x_C + x_D + x_E + x_F \leftarrow eq.1$$

Eq.1 computes the number of staff needed to meet the work demand.

$$x_F + x_A \geq d_A \leftarrow ieq.1$$

(with $d_A=5$)

Ieq.1 states the number of staff who begin on shifts F and A must meet or exceed the work demand of 5.

$$x_F + x_A \geq 5$$

$x_F=0 \qquad x_A=5$

assumed values

$$x_A = 5$$

We'll assign $x_A = 5$, and temporarily assume $x_F = 0$. This assignment will meet the shift A constraint

$$x_A + x_B \geq d_B \leftarrow ieq.2$$

Ieq.2 is the work demand constraint for shift B. Solve ieq.2 for x_B.

104

Solution #32 (cont.)

$$x_B \geq d_B - x_A$$

$d_B = 8 \quad x_A = 5$

Since we're trying to determine the minimum number of workers, assign x_B to 3, the minimum number of staff to begin on shift B which will satisfy the work demand constraint of ieq. 2.

$$x_B \geq 8 - 5$$

$$x_B \geq 3$$

$x_B = 3$

$$x_B = 3$$

Use ie. 3, ie. 4 and ie. 5 to solve for x_C, x_D and x_E the same way we solved for x_B.

$$x_B + x_C \geq d_C \leftarrow ieq. 3$$

$$x_C \geq d_C - x_B$$

$d_C = 15 \quad x_B = 3$

$$x_C \geq 15 - 3$$

$$x_C \geq 12$$

$$x_C = 12$$

$$x_C + x_D \geq d_D \leftarrow ieq. 4$$

$$x_D \geq d_D - x_C$$

$d_D = 19 \quad x_C = 12$

$$x_D \geq 19 - 12$$

$$x_D \geq 7$$

$$x_D = 7$$

$$x_D + x_E \geq d_E \leftarrow ieq. 5$$

$$x_C \geq d_E - x_D$$

$d_E = 12 \quad x_D = 7$

$$x_E \geq 12 - 7$$

$$x_E \geq 5$$

$$x_E = 5$$

$$x_E + x_F \geq d_F \leftarrow ieq. 6$$

$$x_F \geq d_F - x_E$$

$d_F = 6 \quad x_E = 5$

$$x_F \geq 6 - 5$$

$$x_F \geq 1$$

$$x_F = 1$$

Use ieq. 6 to revise variable x_F based on d_F and d_E.

Plug in variables x_A, x_B, x_C, x_D, x_E and x_F into eq. 1, then solve for N.

$x_A = 5 \quad x_C = 12 \quad x_E = 5$

$$N = x_A + x_B + x_C + x_D + x_E + x_F \leftarrow eq. 1$$

$x_B = 3 \quad x_D = 7 \quad x_F = 1$

$$N = 5 + 3 + 12 + 7 + 5 + 1$$

$$N = 33 \qquad \underline{\text{Answer:}} \quad \boxed{B}$$

Civil Engineering Practice Examination #2

Solution #33

Find: Q_B ← the flow rate through pipe BE

Given:

$\left.\begin{array}{l} d=6\,[in] \\ L=10\,[ft] \\ f=0.021 \end{array}\right\}$ the pipe diameter, length and friction coefficient for all 7 pipe segments in the network

$Q=2.41\,[ft^3/s]$ ← the total flow rate into and out of the system

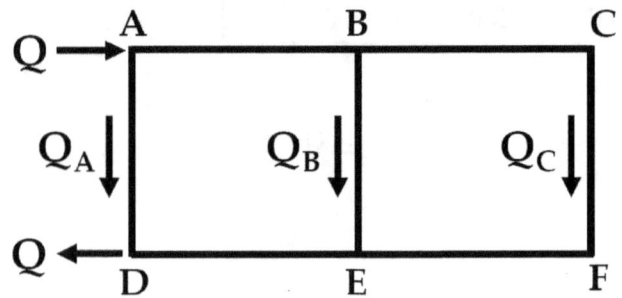

A) $0.346\,[ft^3/s]$

B) $0.599\,[ft^3/s]$

C) $1.011\,[ft^3/s]$

D) $1.464\,[ft^3/s]$

Analysis:

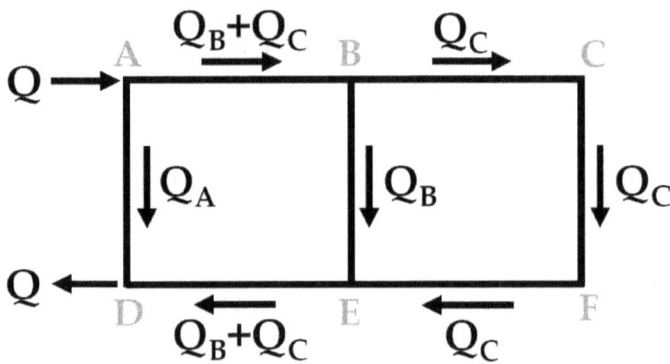

Figure 1

Figure 1 identifies the flow rate through each pipe of the network.

$$Q=Q_A+Q_B+Q_C \leftarrow eq.1$$

Eq.1 computes the total flow through the system.

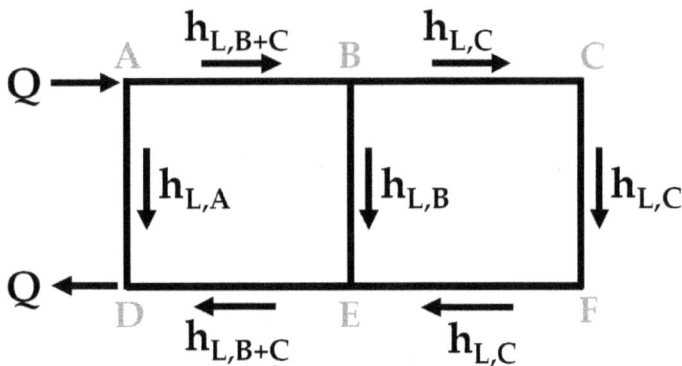

Figure 2

Figure 2 identifies the headloss through each pipe of the network.

Solution #33 (cont.)

Eq. 2 equates the headloss between junctions A and D.

$$h_{L,A}=2*h_{L,B+C}+h_{L,B}=2*h_{L,B+C}+3*h_{L,C} \leftarrow eq.2$$

$$d=6\,[in]*\frac{1}{12}\left[\frac{ft}{in}\right] \leftarrow eq.3$$

Eq. 3 converts the diameter of each pipe to units of feet.

$$d=0.5\,[ft]$$

f=0.021   L=10 [ft]

$$h_L=\frac{f*L*v^2}{2*g*d} \leftarrow eq.4$$

g=32.2 [ft/s²]   d=0.5 [ft]

Eq. 4 computes the headloss through a single pipe segment.

Plug in variables f, L, g and d into eq. 4, then solve for h_L.

$$h_L=\frac{0.021*10[ft]*v^2}{2*32.2\,[ft/s^2]*0.5\,[ft]}$$

$$h_L=6.522*10^{-3}\,[s^2/ft]*v^2 \leftarrow eq.5$$

$$v=Q/A \leftarrow eq.6$$

flow rate   cross-sectional
of the pipe

Eq. 6 computes the velocity of flow through a pipe.

d=0.5 [ft]

$$A=\frac{\pi*d^2}{4} \leftarrow eq.7$$

Eq. 7 computes the cross-sectional area of each pipe.

$$A=\frac{\pi*(0.5\,[ft])^2}{4}$$

Plug in the diameter into eq. 7, then solve for the area.

$$A=0.1964\,[ft^2]$$

Solution #33 (cont.)

$$v = Q/A \leftarrow eq.\,6$$

$$A = 0.1964\,[\text{ft}^2]$$

$$v = Q/0.1964\,[\text{ft}^2]$$

$$v = 5.0916\,[\text{ft}^{-2}] * Q$$

Plug in the area into eq. 6 and simplify.

$$v = 5.0916\,[\text{ft}^{-2}] * Q$$

$$h_L = 6.522*10^{-3}\,[\text{s}^2/\text{ft}] * v^2 \leftarrow eq.\,5$$

Plug in the velocity into eq. 5, then simplify.

$$h_L = 6.522*10^{-3}\,[\text{s}^2/\text{ft}] * (5.0916\,[\text{ft}^{-2}] * Q)^2$$

$$h_L = 0.1691\,[\text{s}^2/\text{ft}^5] * Q^2 \leftarrow eq.\,8$$

From eq. 8, the headloss through each pipe is directly proportional to the flow rate squared.

$$h_{L,A} = 0.1691\,[\text{s}^2/\text{ft}^5] * Q_A^2$$

$$h_{L,B} = 0.1691\,[\text{s}^2/\text{ft}^5] * Q_B^2$$

$$h_{L,C} = 0.1691\,[\text{s}^2/\text{ft}^5] * Q_C^2$$

$$h_{L,B+C} = 0.1691\,[\text{s}^2/\text{ft}^5] * (Q_B + Q_C)^2$$

$$h_{L,B} = 0.1691\,[\text{s}^2/\text{ft}^5] * Q_B^2$$

$$h_{L,B} = 3 * h_{L,C} \leftarrow eq.\,9$$

$$h_{L,C} = 0.1691\,[\text{s}^2/\text{ft}^5] * Q_C^2$$

From eq. 2 and Figure 2, headloss $h_{L,B}$ is three times headloss $h_{L,C}$.

Plug in $h_{L,B}$ and $h_{L,C}$ into eq. 9, then solve for Q_B as a function of Q_C.

$$0.1691\,[\text{s}^2/\text{ft}^5] * Q_B^2 = 3 * 0.1691\,[\text{s}^2/\text{ft}^5] * Q_C^2$$

$$Q_B = 1.732 * Q_C$$

$$Q_C = 0.577 * Q_B$$

Solution #33 (cont.)

$Q_C = 0.577 * Q_B$

$h_{L,B+C} = 0.1691 [s^2/ft^5] * (Q_B + Q_C)^2$ ←eq. 10

Plug in Q_C into eq. 10 and simplify.

$h_{L,B+C} = 0.1691 [s^2/ft^5] * (Q_B + (0.577 * Q_B))^2$

$h_{L,B+C} = 0.4205 [s^2/ft^5] * Q_B^2$

$h_{L,A} = 0.1691 [s^2/ft^5] * Q_A^2$

From eq. 2 and Figure 2, eq. 11 relates headlosses $h_{L,A}$, $h_{L,B}$ and $h_{L,B+C}$.

$h_{L,A} = 2 * h_{L,B+C} + h_{L,B}$ ←eq. 11

$h_{L,B+C} = 0.4205 [s^2/ft^5] * Q_B^2$

Plug in $h_{L,A}$, $h_{L,B}$ and $h_{L,B+C}$ into eq. 11, then solve for Q_A as a function of Q_B.

$h_{L,B} = 0.1691 [s^2/ft^5] * Q_B^2$

$0.1691 [s^2/ft^5] * Q_A^2 = 2 * 0.4205 [s^2/ft^5] * Q_B^2 + 0.1691 [s^2/ft^5] * Q_B^2$

$Q_A = 2.444 * Q_B$

$Q = 2.41 [ft^3/s]$ $Q_C = 0.577 * Q_B$

$Q = Q_A + Q_B + Q_C$ ←eq. 1

Plug in Q, Q_A, and Q_C into eq. 1, then solve for Q_B.

$Q_A = 2.444 * Q_B$

$2.41 [ft^3/s] = 2.444 * Q_B + Q_B + 0.577 * Q_B$

$Q_B = 0.599 [ft^3/s]$

Answer: $\boxed{B}$

Civil Engineering Practice Examination #2

Solution #34

Find: η ← porosity of the soil sample

Given:

$SG = 2.70$ ← specific gravity of the solid material

$\varrho_T = 110 \ [lb/ft^3]$ ← total density of the soil sample

$S = 25\%$ ← saturation

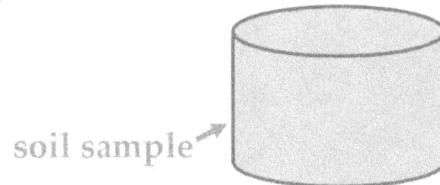

soil sample →

A) 0.16

B) 0.28

C) 0.38

D) 0.62

Analysis:

volume of voids

$$\eta = \frac{V_V}{V_T} \leftarrow eq.1$$

porosity

total volume

Eq.1 computes the porosity of a soil sample.

$$V_T = 1 \ [ft^3]$$

Since no volumes or masses are provided in the problem statement, we'll assume the total volume equals 1 cubic foot.

$$\varrho_T = \frac{M_W + M_S}{V_T} \leftarrow eq.2$$

$\varrho_T = 110 \ [lb/ft^3]$ $V_T = 1 \ [ft^3]$

Eq.2 computes the total unit weight of the soil sample.

Plug in variables ϱ_T and V_T into eq.2, then solve for M_W.

$$110 \ [lb/ft^3] = \frac{M_W + M_S}{1 \ [ft^3]}$$

$$M_W = 110 [lb] - M_S \leftarrow eq.3$$

$S = 25\% = 0.25$

$$S = \frac{V_W}{V_V} \leftarrow eq.4$$

Eq.4 computes the saturation of the soil sample.

$V_T = 1 \ [ft^3]$ $V_V = V_T - V_S$

Plug in variables S and V_V into eq. 4.

$$0.25 * (V_T - V_S) = V_W \leftarrow eq.5$$

Plug in variable V_T into eq. 5.

Solution #34 (cont.)

$$V_W = M_W / \varrho_W$$

$$0.25*(1\,[\text{ft}^3] - V_S) = V_W \;\leftarrow eq.\,6$$

$$V_S = M_S / (SG*\varrho_W)$$

Plug in the equations for V_S and V_W into eq. 6.

$$M_W = 110\,[\text{lb}] - M_S$$

$$0.25\,[\text{ft}^3] - 0.25 * \frac{M_S}{SG*\varrho_W} = \frac{M_W}{\varrho_W} \;\leftarrow eq.\,7$$

$$SG = 2.70 \qquad \varrho_W = 62.4\,[\text{lb/ft}^3]$$

Plug in variables SG, M_W, and ϱ_W into eq. 7, then solve for M_S.

$$0.25\,[\text{ft}^3] - 0.25 * \frac{M_S}{2.70*62.4\,[\text{lb/ft}^3]} = \frac{110\,[\text{lb}] - M_S}{62.4\,[\text{lb/ft}^3]} \;\leftarrow eq.\,8$$

$$M_S = 104.0\,[\text{lb}]$$

$$M_S = 104.0\,[\text{lb}]$$

$$V_S = \frac{M_S}{SG*\varrho_W} \;\leftarrow eq.\,8$$

$$SG = 2.70 \qquad \varrho_W = 62.4\,[\text{lb/ft}^3]$$

Plug in variables SG, M_S, and ϱ_W into eq. 8, then solve for V_S.

$$V_S = \frac{104.0\,[\text{lb}]}{2.70*62.4\,[\text{lb/ft}^3]}$$

$$V_S = 0.617\,[\text{ft}^3]$$

$$V_V = V_T - V_S \;\leftarrow eq.\,9$$

$$V_T = 1\,[\text{ft}^3] \qquad V_S = 0.617\,[\text{ft}^3]$$

Eq. 9 computes the volume of voids in the soil sample.

Plug in variables V_T and V_S into eq. 9, then solve for V_V.

$$V_V = 1\,[\text{ft}^3] - 0.617\,[\text{ft}^3]$$

$$V_V = 0.383\,[\text{ft}^3]$$

Solution #34 (cont.)

$V_V = 0.383 \, [\text{ft}^3]$

$$\eta = \frac{V_V}{V_T} \leftarrow eq.\,1$$

$V_T = 1 \, [\text{ft}^3]$

Plug in the values of V_V and V_T into eq. 1, then solve for η.

$$\eta = \frac{0.383 \, [\text{ft}^3]}{1 \, [\text{ft}^3]}$$

$$\eta = 0.383$$

Answer: $\boxed{\text{C}}$

Solution #35

Find: G_1 ← the approach grade of the vertical curve

Given:

$STA_A = 3+50$
$Elev_A = 141.8$ [ft]
$STA_B = 4+50$
$Elev_B = 140.1$ [ft]
$STA_C = 6+00$
$Elev_C = 142.9$ [ft]

the stationing and elevation of points A, B and C on the vertical curve

the vertical curve begins at point A

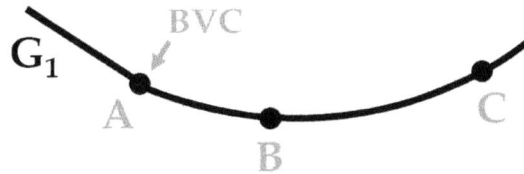

G_1

BVC

A

B

C

A) -1.1%

B) -2.1%

C) -3.1%

D) -4.1%

Analysis:

$$Elev = 0.5*R*x^2 + G_1*x + Elev_{BVC} \leftarrow eq.1$$

rate of grade change

approach grade

BVC = A

Eq. 1 computes the elevation of a point on the vertical curve.

$$Elev_B = 0.5*R*L_{AB}^2 + G_1*L_{AB} + Elev_A \leftarrow eq.2$$

Eq. 2 computes the elevation of point B.

$STA_B = 4+50 = 450$ [ft]

$$L_{AB} = STA_B - STA_A \leftarrow eq.3$$

$STA_A = 3+50 = 350$ [ft]

Eq. 3 computes the horizontal distance between points A and B.

Plug in variables STA_B and STA_A into eq. 3, then solve for L_{AB}.

$$L_{AB} = 450 \text{ [ft]} - 350 \text{ [ft]}$$

$$L_{AB} = 100 \text{ [ft]}$$

$Elev_B = 140.1$ [ft] $Elev_A = 141.8$ [ft]

Plug in variables $Elev_B$, L_{AB} and $Elev_A$ into eq. 2, then simplify.

$$Elev_B = 0.5*R*L_{AB}^2 + G_1*L_{AB} + Elev_A \leftarrow eq.2$$

$L_{AB} = 100$ [ft]

$$140.1 \text{ [ft]} = 0.5*R*(100 \text{ [ft]})^2 + G_1*100 \text{ [ft]} + 141.8 \text{ [ft]}$$

Solution #35 (cont.)

$$5{,}000\,[\text{ft}^2]*R + 100\,[\text{ft}]*G_1 = -1.7\,[\text{ft}] \leftarrow eq.\,4$$

$$\text{Elev}_C = 0.5*R*L_{AC}^2 + G_1*L_{AC} + \text{Elev}_A \leftarrow eq.\,5$$

Eq. 5 computes the elevation of point C.

$STA_C = 6{+}00 = 600\,[\text{ft}]$

$$L_{AC} = STA_C - STA_A \leftarrow eq.\,6$$

$STA_A = 3{+}50 = 350\,[\text{ft}]$

Eq. 6 computes the horizontal distance between points A and C.

Plug in variables STA_C and STA_A into eq. 6, then solve for L_{AC}.

$$L_{AC} = 600\,[\text{ft}] - 350\,[\text{ft}]$$

$$L_{AC} = 250\,[\text{ft}]$$

Plug in variables Elev_C, L_{AC} and Elev_A into eq. 5, then simplify.

$\text{Elev}_C = 142.9\,[\text{ft}]$ $\text{Elev}_A = 141.8\,[\text{ft}]$

$$\text{Elev}_C = 0.5*R*L_{AC}^2 + G_1*L_{AC} + \text{Elev}_A \leftarrow eq.\,5$$

$L_{AC} = 250\,[\text{ft}]$

$$142.9\,[\text{ft}] = 0.5*R*(250\,[\text{ft}])^2 + G_1*250\,[\text{ft}] + 141.8\,[\text{ft}]$$

$$31{,}250\,[\text{ft}^2]*R + 250\,[\text{ft}]*G_1 = 1.1\,[\text{ft}] \leftarrow eq.\,7$$

Solve the linear system of equations from eq. 4 and eq. 7 to solve for R and G.

$$(5{,}000\,[\text{ft}^2]*R + 100\,[\text{ft}]*G_1 = -1.7\,[\text{ft}])*2.5$$

Multiply both sides of eq. 4 by 2.5.

$$12{,}500\,[\text{ft}^2]*R + 250\,[\text{ft}]*G_1 = -4.25\,[\text{ft}] \leftarrow eq.\,8$$

$$31{,}250\,[\text{ft}^2]*R + 250\,[\text{ft}]*G_1 = 1.1\,[\text{ft}] \leftarrow eq.\,7$$
$$-(12{,}500\,[\text{ft}^2]*R + 250\,[\text{ft}]*G_1 = -4.25\,[\text{ft}]) \leftarrow eq.\,8$$

Subtract eq. 8 from eq. 7.

$$18{,}750\,[\text{ft}^2]*R = 5.35\,[\text{ft}] \leftarrow eq.\,9$$

Solve eq. 9 for R.

Solution #35 (cont.)

$$R = 2.8539*10^{-4}[ft^{-1}]$$

Solve eq. 7 for G_1.

$$G_1 = 0.0044 - 125[ft]*R \leftarrow eq. 10$$

$$R = 2.8539*10^{-4}[ft^{-1}]$$

Plug in variable R into eq. 10, then solve for G_1.

$$G_1 = 0.0044 - 125[ft]*2.8539*10^{-4}[ft^{-1}]$$

$$G_1 = -0.03127$$

$$G_1 = -3.13\%$$

Answer: $\boxed{C}$

Civil Engineering Practice Examination #2

Solution #36

Find: $P(EF_C \leq 7)$ ← the probability the early finish of activity C is not later than week 7

Given:

$ES_A = 1$ ← the early start of activity A

$D_A = 2$ ← the duration of activity A

$P(D_B)$ ← probability of duration for activity B and activity C → $P(D_C)$

duration of activity B

duration of activity C

Task	Pred
A	-
B	A
C	B

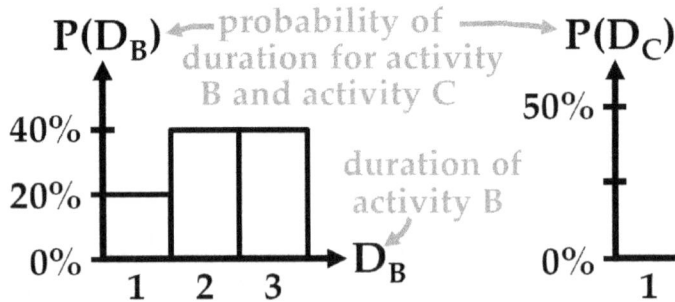

project schedule

time periods are in weeks

A) 10%

B) 20%

C) 40%

D) 60%

Analysis:

Figure 1 identifies the sequence of tasks using the project schedule.

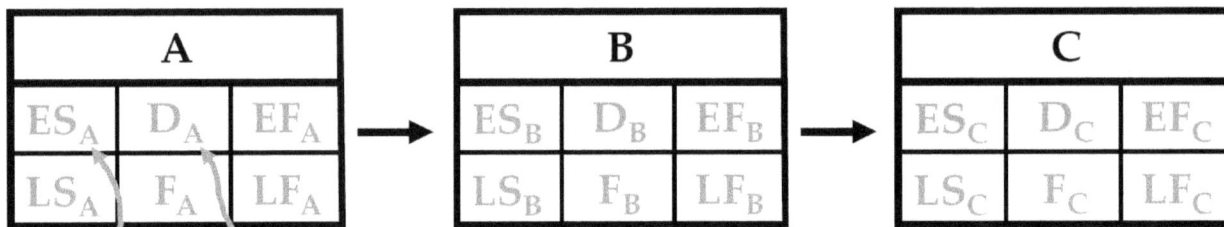

A		
ES_A	D_A	EF_A
LS_A	F_A	LF_A

B		
ES_B	D_B	EF_B
LS_B	F_B	LF_B

C		
ES_C	D_C	EF_C
LS_C	F_C	LF_C

$ES_A = 1$ $D_A = 2$

Figure 1

$$EF_C = ES_B + D_B + D_C \quad \leftarrow eq.1$$

Eq.1 computes the early finish of Activity C.

$ES_A = 1$ $D_A = 2$

$$ES_B = EF_A = ES_A + D_A \quad \leftarrow eq.2$$

Eq.2 computes the early start of Activity B and the early finish of Activity A.

$$ES_B = EF_A = 1 + 2$$

$$ES_B = EF_A = 3$$

Plug in variables ES_A and D_A into eq.1, then solve for ES_B and EF_A.

$ES_B = 3$

$$EF_C = ES_B + D_B + D_C \leftarrow eq.1$$

Plug in ES_B into eq.1, then simplify.

$$EF_C = 3 + D_B + D_C \leftarrow eq.3$$

$EF_C \leq 7$

Replace the early finish of activity C equality with the requirement from the problems statement.

116

Solution #36 (cont.)

$$7 \geq 3 + D_B + D_C$$

$$4 \geq D_B + D_C \leftarrow ieq.1$$

Ieq.1 states the duration of Activity B plus the duration of Activity C must be at most 4.

$$P(EF_C \leq 7) = \sum P(D_B) * P(D_C) \leftarrow eq.4$$

where $D_B + D_C \leq 4$

The probability the early finish is not later than week 7 is the sum product of the probabilities of durations B and C where $D_B + D_C \leq 4$.

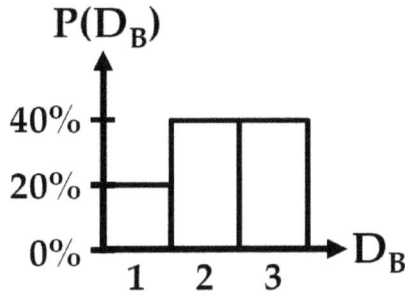

Figure 2

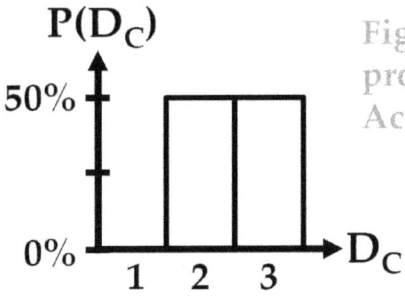

Figure 3

Figure 2 and Figure 3 show the probability of the duration of Activities B and C, respectively.

Table 1 identifies the three outcomes which satisfy ieq.1.

D_B	$P(D_B)$	D_C	$P(D_C)$	$D_B + D_C$	$P(D_B) * P(D_C)$
1	0.2	2	0.5	3	0.1
1	0.2	3	0.5	4	0.1
2	0.4	2	0.5	4	0.2

Table 1

Expand the summation in eq.4 to include all duration combinations which satisfy ieq.1.

$$P(D_B=1) * P(D_C=2) = 0.1$$

$$P(EF_C \leq 7) = P(D_B=1) * P(D_C=2) + P(D_B=1) * P(D_C=2) + P(D_B=2) * P(D_C=2) \leftarrow eq.4$$

$$P(D_B=1) * P(D_C=3) = 0.1 \qquad P(D_B=2) * P(D_C=2) = 0.2$$

$$P(EF_C \leq 7) = 0.1 + 0.1 + 0.2$$

$$P(EF_C \leq 7) = 0.4 = 40\% \qquad \underline{\textbf{Answer:}} \quad \boxed{C}$$

Plug in the probabilities for each row from Table 1 into eq.5, then solve for $P(EF_C \leq 7)$.

Civil Engineering Practice Examination #2

Solution #37

Find: v_c ← the critical velocity

Given: $b=2\,[m]$ ← base width of the rectangular channel

$C_2=0.590$ ← coefficient for the triangular weir

plan view of → channel and weir

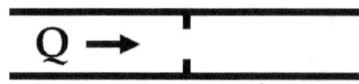

$Q \rightarrow$

$H=1.4\,[m]$ ← total hydraulic head at the triangular weir

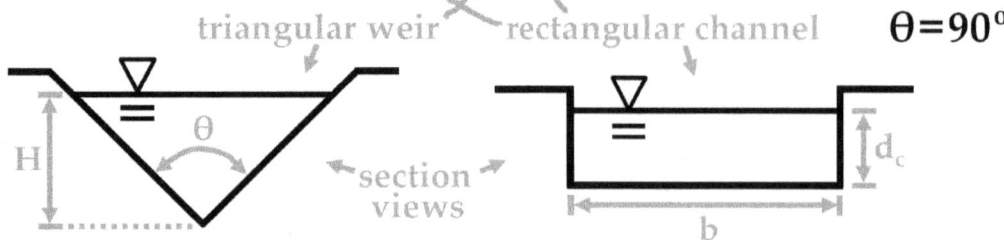

triangular weir ↘ ↙ rectangular channel

$\theta=90°$

section views

b

d_c

A) 0.52 [m/s]

B) 1.04 [m/s]

C) 1.63 [m/s]

D) 2.51 [m/s]

Analysis:

critical velocity $v_c=\sqrt{g*d_c}$ ← eq.1

gravitational acceleration   critical depth

Eq.1 computes the critical velocity in a rectangular channel

critical depth   flow rate

$d_c{}^3=\dfrac{Q^2}{g*b^2}$ ← eq.2

gravitational acceleration   base width

Eq.2 computes the critical depth cubed in a rectangular channel.

$d_c=\left(\dfrac{Q^2}{g*b^2}\right)^{1/3}$ ← eq.3

Solve eq.2 for the critical depth.

Eq.4 computes the flow rate through a triangular weir.

$C_2=0.590$ $\theta=90°$

$Q=C_2*\left(\dfrac{8}{15}\right)*\tan\left(\dfrac{\theta}{2}\right)*\sqrt{2*g}*H^{5/2}$ ← eq.4

$g=9.81\,[m/s^2]$ $H=1.4\,[m]$

Plug in variables C_2, T, g and H into eq.4, then solve for Q.

$Q=0.590*\left(\dfrac{8}{15}\right)*\tan\left(\dfrac{90°}{2}\right)*\sqrt{2*9.81\,[m/s^2]}*(1.4\,[m])^{5/2}$

$Q=3.23\,[m^3/s]$

Solution #37 (cont.)

$Q = 3.23\,[\text{m}^3/\text{s}]$

$$d_c = \left(\frac{Q^2}{g * b^2}\right)^{1/3} \leftarrow eq.3$$

$g = 9.81\,[\text{m/s}^2]$ $b = 2\,[\text{m}]$

Plug in variables Q, g and b into eq.3, then solve for d_c.

$$d_c = \left(\frac{(3.23\,[\text{m}^3/\text{s}])^2}{9.81\,[\text{m/s}^2] * (2\,[\text{m}])^2}\right)^{1/3}$$

$$d_c = 0.643\,[\text{m}]$$

$$v_c = \sqrt{g * d_c} \leftarrow eq.1$$

$g = 9.81\,[\text{m/s}^2]$ $d_c = 0.643\,[\text{m}]$

Plug in variables g and d_c into eq.1, then solve for v_c.

$$v_c = \sqrt{9.81\,[\text{m/s}^2] * 0.643\,[\text{m}]}$$

$$v_c = 2.512\,[\text{m/s}]$$

Answer: $\boxed{\text{D}}$

Civil Engineering Practice Examination #2

Solution #38

<u>Find:</u> C_U ← coefficient of uniformity

<u>Given:</u>

← data from a sieve analysis test

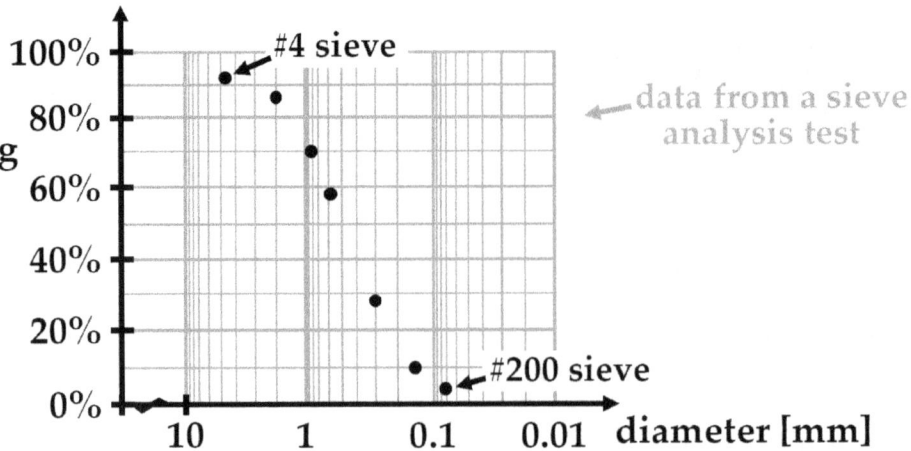

A) 0.7
B) 1.7
C) 4.7
D) 9.8

<u>Analysis:</u>

$$C_U = \frac{D_{60}}{D_{10}} \leftarrow eq.1$$

Eq. 1 computes the coefficient of uniformity.

Figure 1 shows the grain-size distribution plot with a line connecting the data points.

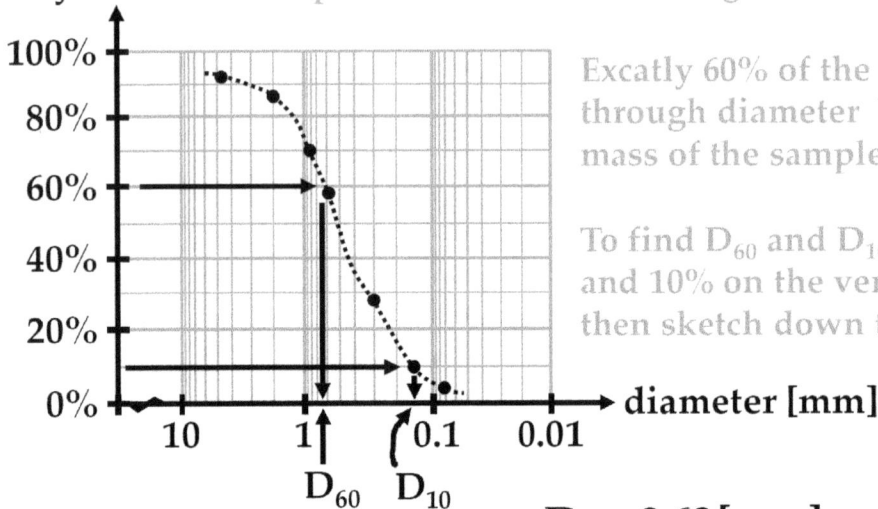

Excatly 60% of the mass of the sample passes through diameter D_{60}, and exactly 10% of the mass of the sample passes through diameter D_{10}

To find D_{60} and D_{10}, sketch over from 60% and 10% on the vertical axis to the curve, then sketch down to the horizontal axis.

$D_{60} = 0.63\,[mm]$ $D_{10} = 0.14\,[mm]$

Figure 1

$D_{60} = 0.63\,[mm]$

$$C_U = \frac{D_{60}}{D_{10}} = \frac{0.63\,[mm]}{0.14\,[mm]} = 4.5 \leftarrow eq.1$$

$D_{10} = 0.14\,[mm]$

Plug in the values for D_{60} and D_{10} into eq. 1, then solve for C_U.

<u>Answer:</u> C

120

Solution #39

<u>Find:</u> v_A ← the maximum vehicle velocity at point A which allows the driver to stop without hitting the object at point B.

<u>Given:</u>

$R=40\,[m]$ ← radius of the horizontal curve

$a=3\,[m/s^2]$

$C_{AB}=70\,[m]$ ← chord length from point A to point B

deceleration of the vehicle when breaking

at point A, the driver first notices the object at point B

$t_r=2.2\,[s]$

reaction time of the driver

A vehicle   object B

C_{AB}

A) 17 [km/hr]

B) 31 [km/hr]

C) 47 [km/hr]

D) 61 [km/hr]

Analysis:

stopping distance → $s_s=s_r+s_b$ ← eq. 1

reaction distance   breaking distance

Eq. 1 computes the stopping distance.

$s_r=v_A*t_r$ ← eq. 2

$t_r=2.2\,[s]$

Eq. 2 computes the reaction distance as the velocity at point A times the reaction time of the driver.

$s_r=2.2\,[s]*v_A$

Plug in variable t_r into eq. 2 then simplify.

$v_B=0\,[m/s]$

$s_b=\dfrac{v_A^2-v_B^2}{2*a}$ ← eq. 3

$a=3\,[m/s^2]$

Eq. 3 computes the breaking distance.

Plug in variables v_B and a into eq. 3, then solve for s_b in terms of v_A.

$s_b=\dfrac{v_A^2-(0)^2}{2*3\,[m/s^2]}$

$s_b=0.167\,[s^2/m]*v_A^2$

curve length → $s_s=L_{AB}=\dfrac{2*\pi*R*I}{360°}$ ← eq. 4

Eq. 4 computes the total stopping distance equal to the length along the curve from point A to point B.

Civil Engineering Practice Examination #2

Solution #39 (cont.)

chord length   interior angle

$$C_{AB} = 2 * R * \sin(I/2) \leftarrow eq.5$$

curve radius

Eq.5 computes the chord length based on the curve radius and interior angle.

$$I = 2 * \sin^{-1}\left(\frac{C_{AB}}{2*R}\right) \leftarrow eq.6$$

$C_{AB} = 70\,[m]$ $R = 40\,[m]$

Solve eq.5 for I.

Plug in variables C_{AB} and R, then solve for I.

$$I = 2 * \sin^{-1}\left(\frac{70\,[m]}{2*40\,[m]}\right)$$

$$I = 122.1°$$

$R = 40\,[m]$ $I = 122.1°$

$$s_s = \frac{2 * \pi * R * I}{360°} \leftarrow eq.4$$

Plug in variables R and I into eq.4, then solve for s_s.

$$s_s = \frac{2 * \pi * 40\,[m] * 122.1°}{360°}$$

$$s_s = 85.24\,[m]$$

$s_b = 0.167\,[s^2/m] * v_A^2$

$s_s = 85.24\,[m] \rightarrow s_s = s_r + s_b \leftarrow eq.1$

$s_r = 2.2\,[s] * v_A$

Plug in variables s_s, s_r and s_b into eq.1, to reduce the equation to 1 unknown variable, v_A.

$$85.24\,[m] = 2.2\,[s] * v_A + 0.167\,[s^2/m] * v_A^2$$

Drop the units and remember v_A has units of meters per second.

$b = 2.2$ $c = -85.24$

$$v_A = \frac{-b \pm \sqrt{b^2 - 4*a*c}}{2*a} \leftarrow eq.7$$

$a = 0.167$

Plug in coefficients a, b and c into the quadratic equation to solve for v_A.

Solution #39 (cont.)

$$v_A = \frac{-2.2 \pm \sqrt{(2.2)^2 - 4*0.167*(-85.24)}}{2*0.167}$$

$$v_A = 16.95\,[\text{m/s}] * 3{,}600\left[\frac{s}{hr}\right] * \frac{1}{1{,}000}\left[\frac{km}{m}\right] \leftarrow eq.8$$

Eq. 8 converts the velocity to units of kilometers per hour.

$$v_A = 61\,[\text{km/hr}]$$

Answer: $\boxed{D}$

Civil Engineering Practice Examination #2

Solution #40

Find: d ← depth to the centroid of the area of steel

Given:

s=1.5[in]

vertical spacing between the two rows of reinforcing bars (edge to edge)

c=2.0[in] ← cover

w=14[in] ← beam width

h=20[in] ← beam height

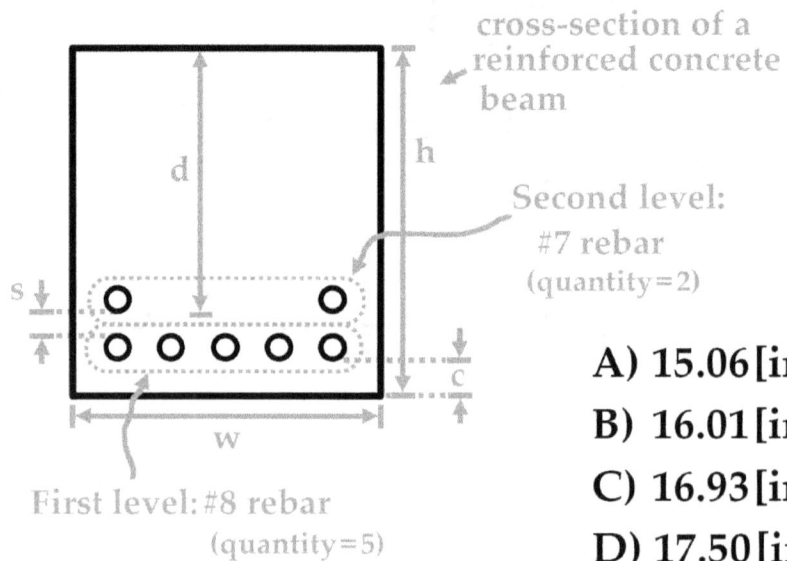

cross-section of a reinforced concrete beam

Second level: #7 rebar (quantity=2)

First level: #8 rebar (quantity=5)

A) 15.06[in]
B) 16.01[in]
C) 16.93[in]
D) 17.50[in]

Analysis:

$$d = \frac{\sum d_i * A_i}{\sum A_i} \leftarrow eq.1$$

depth to the area of steel of level i

area of steel of level i

Eq. 1 computes the depth to the centroid of the area of steel.

$$d = \frac{d_1 * A_1 + d_2 * A_2}{A_1 + A_2} \leftarrow eq.2$$

Expand the summation terms from eq. 1, for 2 levels of rebar.

bar #	Diameter[in]	Area[in²]
6	0.750	0.44
7	0.875	0.60
8	1.000	0.79
9	1.128	1.00

Look up the area of steel for a #7 bar and a #8 bar.

Figure 1 shows the sizes of a few reinforcing bars.

Figure 1

$d_{\#7}=0.875[in]$ $A_{\#7}=0.60[in^2]$

A #7 bar has a diameter of 0.875 in and a cross-sectional area of 0.60 in².

$d_{\#8}=1.000[in]$ $A_{\#8}=0.79[in^2]$

A #8 bar has a diameter of 1.000 in and a cross-sectional area of 0.79 in².

Solution #40 (cont.)

$$A_{\#8}=0.79\,[in^2]$$

$$A_1=5*A_{\#8} \quad \leftarrow eq.3$$

$$A_1=5*0.79\,[in^2]$$

$$A_1=3.95\,[in^2]$$

Eq.3 computes the area of steel on level 1.

Plug in the area of steel for a single #8 rebar into eq.3, then solve for A_1.

$$A_{\#7}=0.60\,[in^2]$$

$$A_2=2*A_{\#7} \quad \leftarrow eq.4$$

$$A_2=2*0.60\,[in^2]$$

$$A_2=1.20\,[in^2]$$

Eq.4 computes the area of steel on level 2.

Plug in the area of steel for a single #7 rebar into eq.4, then solve for A_2.

$$c=2.0\,[in]$$

$$d_1=h-c-0.5*d_{\#8} \quad \leftarrow eq.5$$

$$h=20\,[in] \quad d_{\#8}=1.000\,[in]$$

$$d_1=20\,[in]-2.0\,[in]-0.5*1.000\,[in]$$

$$d_1=17.5\,[in]$$

Eq.5 computes the depth to the area of steel for level 1, which equals the beam height minus the cover, minus half the #8 bar diameter.

Plug in variables h, c and $d_{\#8}$ into eq.5, then solve for d_1.

$$c=2.0\,[in] \quad s=1.5\,[in]$$

$$d_2=h-c-d_{\#8}-s-0.5*d_{\#7} \quad \leftarrow eq.6$$

$$h=20\,[in] \quad d_{\#8}=1.000\,[in] \quad d_{\#7}=0.875\,[in]$$

$$d_2=20\,[in]-2.0\,[in]-1.000\,[in]-1.5\,[in]-0.5*0.875\,[in]$$

$$d_2=15.06\,[in]$$

Eq.6 computes the depth to the area of steel for level 2.

Plug in variables h, c and $d_{\#8}$, s and $d_{\#7}$ into eq.6, then solve for d_2.

Civil Engineering Practice Examination #2

Solution #40 (cont.)

$$d_1 = 17.5 \,[in] \qquad d_2 = 15.06 \,[in]$$

$$d = \frac{d_1 * A_1 + d_2 * A_2}{A_1 + A_2} \leftarrow eq.2$$

$$A_1 = 3.95 \,[in^2] \qquad A_2 = 1.20 \,[in^2]$$

Plug in variables d_1, A_1, d_2 and A_2 into eq.2, then solve for d.

$$d = \frac{17.5 \,[in] * 3.95 \,[in^2] + 15.06 \,[in] * 1.20 \,[in^2]}{3.95 \,[in] + 1.20 \,[in]}$$

$$d = 16.93 \,[in]$$

Answer: $\boxed{C}$

Section 3: Quick Solutions

(page intentionally left blank)

1. D

2. A

3. D

4. B

5. B

6. B

7. D

8. D

9. B

10. B

11. D

12. B

13. D

14. C

15. B

16. C

17. C

18. A

19. A

20. B

21. B

22. A

23. D

24. A

25. A

26. A

27. C

28. C

29. A

30. D

31. C

32. B

33. B

34. C

35. C

36. C

37. D

38. C

39. D

40. C

Notes:

Notes: